I am here at this time, to be an example of connections to Higher realms and beings. I'm showing you my roadmap so you can discover your own.

"You are being summoned, we await your presence at the portal the time is now delay not for what you are about to unveil is of the utmost importance for all humanity. It is time, it is time. Trust in yourself - not Lowell the personality but Lowell whose higher aspect Thoth is waiting for you. Trust you're ready and release all expectations and perceived limitations. Allow your truth to be revealed and then that was the end of the transmission."

Foreward

Beliefs - we all have them

Learn to become an Observer and begin observing yourself.

George Harrison in an interview once said: "you can't believe anything until you have direct perception of it"

With all the chaos around us and your attention for all intents and purposes, stolen from you ... you have formed a series of beliefs based on what you have ingested. These outside influences come with their own agenda and it's rare that they align with your highest good. Over time as you gave away your power, your discernment was thrown out the window and you took in information at a rate too fast to take hold or assimilate, but left a long-lasting belief - one you didn't necessarily choose.

I believe in my own Sovereignty and according to the Law of One - the sovereignty of everyone else I'm connected to as well.

That's every sentient being. I didn't believe it was my place to influence anyone else without being invited to do so. So as all this wisdom and contact with Higher Beings was coming into focus, I wondered - who was I to interrupt someone else's journey? I will tell you now that after sequestering for most of the last part of 2023 - those Higher Beings are almost demanding that I share what I know and share the abilities I have in order for others to see that they can achieve the same level of consciousness.

So I AM going to give you something else to believe in - multidimensionality. Let's start there - it IS a thing so let's get started comprehending how it affects you.

3D background
- Service industry

TIA
- triggered awareness and my vibration level

Meditation
- health benefits
- Healing

Sacred medicine
- ayahuasca journeys

Cosmic cycle
- solar influence from the Central Sun
- Changes in earth's consciousness

Multidimensional experiences
- Telos and the Lemurians
- Kumu and the Light beings
- Thoth wisdom integration
- (Evidentiary Medium) Bringing through inner earth images
- Time dilation on Faery Falls hike
- Activating energetic places (identifying Golden Taya allotments)
- Light beings on a ranch near Sedona

Chosen
- why me
- Experiencer
- Who am I (past lives)

- Abilities restored: bilocation, telepathy, clairvoyance, dimensional straddling, empathic connections, energy manipulation and activation

Observer Recorder Activator

Background

I grew up on the east side of St. Paul Minnesota. I was the oldest of three siblings at the time, and at the age of four, my father divorced my mother, and got custody of myself and my two younger sisters. I would live with my paternal grandparents until I reached 11 which time my father remarried, and we would go on add two more siblings. Before this time I'd have little contact with my natural mother and I had a father that I didn't really get along with. I would learn much later in life that I chose those incarnation circumstances as I wasn't going to need a lot of parenting. I was smart. In the third grade back then, we were given aptitude tests, and I would later learn that my score was the second highest in the entire city. I was a pretty good athlete, and loved the game of hockey so much so that it seemed as though my career trajectory was leading me to become an NHL official. All along my school years, I seemed to be able to navigate my way through all the groups - jocks, geeks, brains, and the kids from the other side of the tracks - I got along with all of them.

I'd move out when I turned 18 and move to Minneapolis. Through a series of circumstances, I would find myself turning down the opportunity to officiate in the NHL and took a job as a desk clerk at a hotel, Sofitel in Bloomington, Minnesota. 90 days after that job began, I would find myself in hospitality management, and would remain there for the next four decades. I would still find the time to officiate hockey games at the local level up through college and semi pro but as a service to others being, My path would follow the hotel business until the early 90s when a health crisis in the family required me to relocate back to Florida without a job.

I had always had an interest in computers, and as it turned out I started doing small projects for people in the neighborhood, and those efforts would grow into an IT business that would sustain itself for 10 years. I would return to the hotel business and for a five-year period I would be able to do both.

During this period I had two sources of income producing six figures each with a house in Florida on a canal with direct access to the Gulf of Mexico. Then hurricane Charlie would take it all away just that quickly the resort would be closed for a minimum of six months, my IT business as I worked out of my home would be unsustainable, and my home itself was damaged by the storm and I would be displaced for 11 months during a time when my wife was going through cancer therapy.

After her passing, I would return to the hotel business for employers I had worked for previously, I would work on a few different renovation projects, and eventually end up in Santa Rosa, California. When that property was sold to another company three years later, I decided I tired of the relocation with new opportunities. I had already lived in nine states, so I decided to stay in Sonoma County, where the climate was better than any place overall in the nation, and I would begin to consult. Here is where I would begin to do consulting with casino properties, managing all the non-gaming operations. The first one of which would be in Baton Rouge, Louisiana. Two years after that, I would return to Sonoma County and consult on a couple of other resort projects until late 2015. I had always enjoyed good health, but I was suffering some unsettling symptoms and it turned out, I suffered from a TIA (a mini stroke) and had surgery the first weekend in December to correct the situation.

Here is where my connection to Higher states of consciousness would trigger. My surgeon had informed me that the recovery would last about 30 days and he had suggested meditation as one method of therapy. I had always been interested in meditation, but I'd never been able to reach that state of peace, quiet and serenity that I was told you could reach. The next few weeks I would research everything on the Internet I could find about meditation, and the one thing I couldn't seem to find was this "mantra" that kept being referred to. And then, one day while I was lying on the couch, I decided to watch The Secret for the third time.

My attention would be drawn to TM - Transcendental Meditation that was mentioned in the program. Other things in my life would also start to line up a path to the metaphysical side of myself, and open access to higher realms of awareness.

Meditation

Now learning to meditate through the Transcendental Meditation process is the same for every initiate. The method by which each individual is taught was handed down by the Maharishi, who received it from his teacher. And TM trainers are not on every corner. Upon reflection, I'm not surprised at all by the synchronicity that there was a trainer who lived about a mile from where I was at the time. I enrolled in the four consecutive day course, and after the second day, I could feel the benefits of this process. Most notably was a sensation that I carried in my belly that I thought was indigestion that would flare up from time to time. What I would notice by day three was that sensation disappeared and that it was actually stress that I was carrying. To this day, I have not suffered from that sensation again. I could discern the differences between meditating by myself, and meditating, even in small groups - the more people's intentions were in harmony, the more powerful the force seem to be. I could clearly see the benefits of meditation and believe that everyone should be exposed to this method. I believed my future was to be a TM trainer. The universe would go onto show me it had different ideas for me.

I do want to point out some healing benefits meditation had for me over time. I have had a history of high blood pressure and that was gone after a few months. Having been an athlete I had some arthritic joint discomfort that also disappeared. I began to eat differently based on what I was craving and over a 90 day period somehow 35 pounds had found itself elsewhere. My joints felt like I was in my early 20s when my physicality was probably at its peak. I didn't diet and watch what I ate. I didn't join a Health club, but somehow that weight just disappeared, and my physical being felt better than I could recall ever. I credit meditation as improving my health to such a degree that I haven't needed medical attention nor seen a doctor of any kind since the TIA incident in December 2015.

I never considered myself much of a book reader, but I started to read volumes of books and watch hours of YouTube videos, having to do with the metaphysical side of ourselves. If there was a way for me to contact God/Spirit, I wanted to experience it for myself.

The First Rabbit Hole - Understanding the Cosmic Cycles

Here is where science helped me comprehend the galactic reason behind Earth's rise in consciousness.

The Galactic Photon Belt Alignment

In 1961 astronomers discovered, by means of satellite instrumentation, what appeared to be an unusual nebula. We normally understand the nebula phenomenon as a vast cloud-like mass of gas or dust. This one, however, appeared to have anomalous properties and was named the Golden Nebula.

What is this electromagnetic cloud, this golden nebula? Its more universal designation is 'photon belt' or 'photon band', consisting of many bands. Any encounter with this belt is recognized by extraterrestrials and advanced galactic civilizations as of great import. The more enlightened ETs refer to the photon belt as a 'planetary trouble shooter'. Planet Earth was in trouble from the damage incurred by our civilization and called for the photon belt—a typical emergency call procedure for planets. But before we look at the Photon Belt in detail, let us cover some background information first.

Cycles of Creation

Our Earth rotates around our Sun, taking approximately 365 days for one complete revolution.

Then our Sun (our entire Solar System, to be exact) rotates around Alcyone, the brightest star of the Pleiades constellation. One complete revolution of our Solar System around Alcyone takes approximately 26,000 years.

In addition, Alcyone and our Solar System are revolving around the Galactic Core (central region) or our Milky Way Galaxy. One complete revolution takes approximately 225 million years.

The Photon Belt

The Photon Belt is the Galactic Plane alignment of hundreds of billions of Milky Way star systems. Our solar system orbits across this Photon Belt twice in approximately 26,000 years (Precession of Equinox).

This 'Great Crossing' thus occurs every 13,000 years. The 'Great Purification' naturally occurring at this time is the result of the surge in brilliant photonic light from the Greater Central Sun out through the conduit of the Galactic Plane Photon Belt.

There are times during our 26,000 year revolution around Alcyone, that our Solar System sits either partly or fully within the Photon Belt (referred to as periods of Light) and greater periods of time where our Solar System is not within this Photon Belt (referred to as periods of Darkness).

Due to the thickness of the Photon Belt's field, we spend 2,000 years in the 'Light', then 11,000 years in 'Darkness' then 2,000 years in 'Light' and then 11,000 years in 'Darkness' – making up our full 26,000 year cycle.

Thus every 13,000 years we reach the PEAK central region of the photon-belt of light and this coincides with the 13,000 year Stellar Cycle of our Sun.

Movement of Our Solar System into the Photon Belt

Our Solar System is now moving into Pleiades Photon Belt once again, into another 2,000 years of 'Light'. In December Solstice 2012, our Solar System has fully entered within this Photon Belt field. Likewise, Earth is now entirely within the photon belt.

It has been intensifying for decades, changing the atmospheres on all the planets in our solar system and accelerating the rate of change in human consciousness. The global evolution revolution in consciousness with the computer/Internet revolution has actually been in resonance with the surging intelligence in the Source Field.

This photonic energy is the highest form of light that is known – the light of Source, carrying a sentient supra-conscious intelligence, coded in the frequencies just as laser light through fiber optics can carry thousands of videos and phone conversations coded in the light. Modern science has only recently 'rediscovered' what the ancients already knew. This understanding of 'Galactic Light' was known anciently to the Gnostics:

The 2000 year old Gnostic text, discovered in Nag Hammadi Egypt in 1945, reveals the cosmic understanding that the brilliant light plasma at the central core of our Galaxy is actually a sentient intelligence.

Furthermore, these Gnostic texts tell us that the physical world we inhabit came into form as the intelligent expression of the plasma light, or 'ether', spiraling out from the Galactic Central Sun." ~ excerpt from Galactic Light

Leading experts of both quantum science and the Mayan Calendar are saying that our DNA will be "upgraded" (coded with intelligence) from the center of our Galaxy – the 'Greater Central Sun'.

Stellar Activations Cycle
The stellar activations have already begun and will continue through 2012 to 2017. This is explained in detail in Ashayana Deane's

Voyagers II: Secrets of Amenti. The principle time cycle is 26,556 years, which is the precession of the equinoxes and is caused by a slow wobble of the Earth as it spins and orbits around the Sun. This is known by astronomers.

Stellar activation occurs when our solar system lines up with the higher frequency bands of Pleiades (star Alcyone), Sirius, Arcturus, Orion and Andromeda. The frequency bands then merge and pass through Earth. If Earth is out of balance within itself due to abuse from invader ETs, the Cabal, and humankind's behavior, the higher frequencies will cause an 'Armageddon'.

To understand the alignment, one could think of circles within circles (cycles within cycles) turning at different rates to which are attached magnets. Clearly, periodically they could line up, forming one long and powerful magnet. This would act like a powerful current. It is called a holographic beam since it contains the fundamental energy of these systems.

After the convergence, this holographic beam carries the remains of photon activity. When Earth is in alignment, it merges with higher dimensional parallel Earth, Tara. During this process the particles and antiparticles of these planets and their antiparallel planets are unified in certain specific ways. When these particles and antiparticles come together they create intense photonic activity which we know as the Photon Belt. It is continually renewed each cycle as the holographic beam passes out through Alcyone, leaving the band around this star.

What Does This All Mean For Planet Earth?
By the solstice of 21 December 2016, our entire solar system has entered fully in the Photon Band of Light, receiving direct energetic transmissions from Alcyone and from our Galactic Core of the Milky Way – The Waves of Love.

In addition, we are also coming to the end of the Grand Cycle of time, the end of another 225 million year cycle, 26,000 year cycle and 365 day cycle. Thus on this December solstice there was a grand alignment in our stellar skies of the Galactic Core of the Milky Way, with Alcyone, with our Sun and with Earth – marking the end of some significant cycles of time (or frequencies of consciousness).

The Greater Central Sun (Galactic Core) is directly pulsing electromagnetic Wave of Love vibrations though our Central Sun (Alcyone), through our Sun and into Earth, bringing through very high pulsations or frequencies of light energy to Earth.

This electromagnetic energy is facilitating a shift in consciousness, a divine shift of the level of awareness of humanity from an egoic third dimensional state of fear, to a consciousness level of Love and Oneness, a fifth dimensional state of being.

The Galactic Center
The Galactic Center is 26,000 Light Years from the Sun, and we are merging with it now as we come to the end of the cycle. It is the cross over point, the Void, Zero Point and our Solar System is moving through it as the end of the Mayan Calendar.

According to the Maya and many other cosmic cultures, the Galactic Center is where souls pass after death, and re-birthed, where time and space have collapsed totally and do not exist. It is the impulse from the Void; the universe pulses out creating life and flows in creating transformation, the cross over place.

The Galactic Center is a gateway of change. It opens us up to multidimensional spaces and we can access our past and future all NOW in holograms of light. The Galactic Center emits massive amounts of infra-red rays which activate us to remember our true radiance and light and ground it within us, as we open up to our multidimensional Self and bodies of Light.

The official thought is that the Galactic Center is a super-massive Black Hole. Scientists do not look at it from a multidimensional perspective but just a third dimensional one. They fear all is lost in a Black Hole when in actual fact everything just unifies and merges, returns through the Black Hole and then out through a White Hole of another prism of Creation.

The Galactic Center is the cross over point, black hole where we move through as we complete Duality and unify.

Zero Point

Gregg Braden is currently traveling around the United States and in the media, telling of the scientific proof of the Earth passing through the Photon Belt and the slowing of the Earth's rotation. At the same time there is an increase in the resonant frequency of the Earth (Schumann Resonance). When the Earth stops its rotation and the resonance frequency reaches 13 cycles, we will be at a zero-point magnetic field. The Earth will be stopped, and in 2 or 3 days it will start turning again in the opposite direction. This will produce a reversal in the magnetic fields around the Earth and so forth.

Geophysical Condition #1: Earth's Rising Base Frequency

Earth's background base frequency, or "heartbeat" (called Schumann Resonance, or

SR) is rising dramatically. Though it varies among geographical regions, for decades the overall measurement was 7.8 cycles per second. This was once thought to be a constant; global military communications developed on this frequency. Recent reports set the rate at over 11 cycles, and climbing. Science does not know why, or what to make of it. Gregg Braden found data collected by Norwegian and Russian researchers on this; it's not widely reported in the U.S.

Geophysical Condition #2: Earth's Diminishing Magnetic Field

While Earth's "pulse-rate" is rising, her magnetic field strength, on the other hand, is declining. According to Professor Bannerjee of the University of New Mexico, the field has lost up to half of its intensity in the last 4,000 years.

Time will appear to speed up. A 24-hour day will seem to be about 16 hours or less. Remember the Schumann Resonance (or "heart-beat" of Mother Earth) has been 7.8 cycles for thousands of years, but has been rising since 1980. It is about 12 cycles at the present. It stops at 13 cycles.

Zero Point or the Shift of the Ages has been predicted by ancient peoples for thousands of years.

Photon Energy
Photons are the smallest possible particles of light in quantum physics. A photon particle is the result of a collision between an anti-electron or positron and an electron. These split second collisions cause the charges of the particles to cancel and the resultant mass is converted into energy in the form of photons.

Photons are emitted during the transmission of one energy state to another. They have zero mass and no electrical charge. Photons are what the ancients harnessed as energy for communication, stellar travel, energy production etc.

Photon promises to be a major source for our energy requirements in the very near future. Photon energy will provide a new and unlimited source of energy. The energy source will enable our world to easily abandon the fossil fueled industrial age. In a short period of time, our civilization can begin to rid itself of those technologies that have polluted our planet for the past two and one half centuries.

Photon energy will not only provide our bodies with a maximum efficiency of energy use, it will also do the same for our homes and factories. We will enter a new and wondrous energy age. There is also an additional benefit to this event. Space travel will become simple and the preferred mode of transportation.

In aboriginal mythology it is often stated that humans were different then than they are now and that they had a bridge to the stars. In the Photon Belt, we will be different and with the power provided by the photon beam as a propulsion system the planets and the stars will become quite near. Soon, it will be as easy to travel to Sirius or any nearby star as it is now to travel to New York.

Transformation of Consciousness

Being in the Photon Belt will play a significant role in the transformation of humankind. Both great illumination of consciousness will occur as well as great resistance to new ideas. This is a period of awakening essentially due to the ascension cycle and planetary alignment.

The phenomenon of both the Photon Belt plus stellar activity will reduce the veil stopping us from seeing who we are. It will remove some of the barriers around cells and DNA making them more reactive or responsive to new energies, and in fact the DNA will attempt to respond to the changing frequencies, increasing its capacity.

It presents opportunities for change on a planet by adding new energies. It increases the flow of energy in the magnetic grids of Earth, attracting new ideas and energies. People will feel the need to transform but those who consider this physical reality their only expression will dwindle into greater fixations, blocks and negativity.

The Guardians, IAFW and Emerald Covenant Angelic Nations

The Interdimensional Association of Free Worlds (IAFW) was formed 250 billion years ago to serve the role of primary Guardian Race Administration and protectors of the Emerald Covenant freedom agendas in our 15-dimensional Time Matrix.

Throughout the many eons of intergalactic, interdimensional history, the IAFW and its countless Emerald Covenant Guardian Angelic Nations, continually labor to restore and maintain the structural integrity of our Time Matrix. Presently there are over 25 billion different interdimensional, interstellar Nations serving as active members of the IAFW.

The Guardians' association spans many different planetary, star systems, space, time and dimensions. Membership within the Guardians organization encompasses the matter-based galaxies and universes of the lower dimensions to the immeasurable cosmic reality fields of pure consciousness free from dimensional structure. They work together to assist in the evolution of developing cultures throughout the multidimensional Universe.

Between 2017 and 2022, when the Halls of Amenti (the blue sphere holding our divine blueprints) merge Tara and Earth together, those humans and Indigos who have assembled the fifth DNA strand and are eligible for ascension to Tara will be guided to interdimensional transportation locations to Tara. Those who have assembled the sixth and seventh strands may be transported to Gaia. There may be others who will be transported to their home planets or elsewhere where they play and celebrate with their Family of Consciousness. Remaining Angelic Humans and Indigos will progress in their 12 Code activation and DNA blue print activation.

Angelic humans and the races of Earth will soon be prepared for visits from the Inner Earth Eieyani, Sirius B Maharaji, Azurite and other Emerald Covenant Races. The Guardians will invite ethical Earth groups to join the Emerald Covenant, where spiritually mature and virtuous humans would be offered the opportunity to reclaim their role as guardians of the Planetary Templar Complex. The first physical contacts of the Emerald Covenant Angelic Nations is scheduled between 2017 and 2022; these contacts will be made individually and privately.

Role of the Galactic Federation of Light
The Galactic Federation of Light was founded over 4.5 million years ago to prevent inter-dimensional dark forces from dominating and exploiting this galaxy.

At present, there are just over 200,000 member star nations, confederations or unions. Approximately 40% are humanoids and the rest are varied forms of sentient beings. Most members of the Galactic Federation are fully conscious beings.
The Galactic Federation's purpose is to foster goodwill and understanding of the star nations that are answering the call of Earth's Spiritual Hierarchy to assist us in our ascension/transformation process.

Andromeda M31 Galaxy

The Andromeda M31 Galaxy is interfacing with our Milky Way Galaxy and holds very high frequencies of unified matrix of light. This is aligning us back to the higher dimensional Solar System. This is the Solar System of the Greater Central Sun, which is Sirius B, a great star that has a Solar System so vast that the Solar System of the Central Sun Alcyone is on an outer orbit of it, and our Solar System is on an outer orbit of Alcyone's Solar System. The Blue Star refers to Sirius B from the Hopi Prophecy.

Our galaxy will gradually merge and rejoin the Andromeda Galaxy, from which it fell out of eons ago.

There is a loop that we jump in order to move into the higher dimensional Solar System and in order to do that we have to shift our consciousness. For as we align with the Sun, the Second Sun, Central Sun and Greater Central Sun, we awaken the Sun within us and the Earth herself becomes a Sun (within the next one thousand years in linear time). This is the dimensional shift, the Golden Age we are moving into. This is happening whether we like it or not. It is the completion of three grand Cycles, and is like trying to stop night and day from happening. So we open to the flow and move with it, or resist in fear and stay stuck in the third dimension for eons more time.

The Sun, Central Sun and Greater Central Sun

The Sun is connected to every aspect of life and creates the world as we live in it. The Sun is not just a gaseous ball but has very highly evolved worlds and Beings. The Sun is a great place of learning and wisdom as well as a stage of initiation for those who choose to go through the Sun and beyond.

The Sun is connected to the Central Suns. There are many Suns and Central Suns; it is through these Suns that all worlds are created and aligned. The Sun illuminates the vibrations that help us to grow. If it feels our Love, it feeds that Love; if it feels our fear, it creates experiences for us to open up more fully to Love.

The Sun is Light, and the Light allows us to see that which is not light, our separation and duality. We are given the gift of seeing our polarities to unify.

As we align with our Sun, it sends out cosmic rays and solar flares. These cosmic rays also come from other Suns and Central Suns that are aligning with the Earth as we star map the grid with the solar system in harmony once more. The last time we were aligned to the Sun and Central Sun was in the last Golden Age. At that time we created the pyramids, stone circles, standing stones in alignment with different stars in our Solar System. These stars are Suns and Central Suns.

The Greater Central Sun is now also aligning with us which means all these high frequencies of Source energy are creating a shift in consciousness.

We can only access the energy of the Greater Central Sun when our hearts are open and we operate from love in our connection to the Source. Once we have loved and accepted our negative emotions and thoughts, we have the ability to fully love our self with all our imbalances and karma. As we surrender to Divine Will, we come to peace within. Love, compassionate, acceptance and allowing become our natural state of Being.

This is happening more and more; many have or are reaching this state of love and allowing. Your love sets you free, and you move into the higher dimensional realms as the Greater Central Sun illuminates you from your heart and eternal connection to the Source within.

Liquid Light Plasma
We have been reborn. Love has transformed enough of the fear for us to move into the Golden Age in Love, Peace and Joy. We are awakening to our Divine Blueprint and our Divine Birthright and shine the Sun that we are.

Liquid Light Plasma is now flowing freely through the Inner Earth Sun. This upgrade is affecting all of us. We receive the Light through the Pineal and process it all in the Pituitary and the Thymus, regulating our body and Kundalini flow. We are receiving this information from matter, antimatter and dark plasma.

Our multidimensional bodies are Liquid Light Plasma and exist in the worlds of what scientists call dark matter or antimatter, that is lighter and higher frequency than dense matter and interfaces with the higher dimensions. As this process evolves within us our DNA, RNA and Light Bodies activate to hold greater light and our energy field is strong and clear. It also means that we have a lot of energy at our disposal, and we must be aware of our thoughts, words and actions. We have a lot of responsibility to be aligned with Source and come from unity, rather than separation consciousness and to take responsibility for all levels of our being.

There is scientific evidence from NASA of a type of magnetic rope of plasmic filaments that acts as a transmission across interplanetary and interstellar space coming from the Galactic Center. This signifies a multidimensional doorway. As we become more Liquid Light Plasmic, we travel in our body through the love of our open heart into the multidimensional realms of existence. Now, as we have completed the old great cycle, we move through the Galactic Center and into the higher dimensional Earth and New Solar System. We become a Sun, as the Sun becomes a Central Sun, and the Central Sun a Greater Central Sun.

Higher Dimensional Earth and New Solar System

The Central Sun in our Solar System is Alcyone, the brightest star in the Pleiadian System, and our Solar System rotates around it in a cycle of approximately 26,000 years. We are coming to the end of this cycle now as we merge through the Galactic Center. The Central Sun revolves around the Greater Central Sun, Sirius B. As our Solar System moves through the Galactic Center, it aligns us with the Central Sun and Greater Central Sun. We become the Sun of our True Self.

It has taken us on a journey of experiencing the levels of creation from the densest levels of consciousness to the highest we can achieve in the Template of Duality. Now we are moving through into the realms of the unified matrix or Template of Oneness and the higher dimensional realms of existence. We are ready to make the big leap, across the gap and into the new Solar System and New Earth.

The Second Sun and the New Solar System

The new Solar System is not so much new but at a higher dimension than the Solar System we inhabit at present. Our Sun was birthed out of this with its binary Twin Sun. Eventually after much interference in the Universe by exploding worlds, wars, comets and deluge of meteorites, our Solar System was created through the density and chaos of these occurrences at a lower frequency than it had once held.

Duality became the norm. The Sun had lost its Twin whose orbit was way out in a cycle of millions of years and separation was the theme. Now as these cycles are completing and the Twin returns, union takes place and the doorway is open through humanity's hearts. Unified with its Twin, the Sun opens the doorway for the shift in frequency back into the higher frequency Solar System it once came from. The music of the spheres are dancing and illuminating the rays of harmonic vibrations to draw us home. As we move into the new Solar System we come home unto ourselves.

The Earth Becomes a Sun

As we align with the Sun, the Second Sun, Central Sun and Greater Central Sun, we awaken the Sun within us and the Earth herself becomes a Sun. Earth becoming a Sun is a gradual process and will come to fruition within the next thousand years in linear time. This is the dimensional shift, the Golden Age we are moving into.

Realignment of the Stars

Planet Earth is now being influenced by entirely new star patternings that we have never before experienced. The influence of these new star patternings will grow in importance in the times to come. This is of great significance and its effects are only beginning to be understood.

There is a constant shifting in the heavens which is creating profound changes. As you know, space is not flat. It curves and bends, containing pockets and folds. These pockets and folds are slowly moving and changing shape. As they do, new pockets are formed and previously sealed-off pockets are opened.

Thus we shall discover that unknown star fields, previously hidden in pockets and folds in space are now slowly being revealed.

Conversely, many star field frequency patternings to which Earth has long been accustomed, are slowly being withdrawn. They are being recalled into newly created pockets and folds in deep space.

This is of tremendous importance for it is part of the establishment of the new etheric blueprint and grid matrix overlay.

Since the Realignment of the Stars actually began long ago, some of these changes have already been observed in the night sky by our astronomers. It has simply taken this long for the changes to be visible due to the slow speed that light travels. While we wait for science to catch up to metaphysics to supply the physical "proof" that some people require, we are already being affected by this shift.

We are experiencing this influx of new star field energies as part of the heightened acceleration of the Time of Completion.

They are helping bring in the accelerated frequencies which are aiding our process of restructurization and recalibration as we make the quantum leap into Oneness.

New Galaxies Interfacing with Milky Way
A Galactic Gate is vaster than a Star Gate and encompasses new seedings of not only the New Earth, new Suns and new Solar System. Since the shift through the Galactic Plane in December 2012 Solstice, stars not from this Milky Way have interchanged with the Milky Way, our galaxy. When the shift happened everything could be likened to 'moving inside out', and there are new Galaxies interfacing with ours.

This is a positive thing as it brings in new energies that are vibrating in higher octaves of light that we are able to hold since we are more in the unified field and unity consciousness, Oneness with all life.

The energies of the new stars feel divine, such gentle soft starlight illuminating to us and from within us. They open pathways to Love, peace within, unity and Oneness.

Sacred medicine

In Feb 2018, I had the opportunity to participate in a weekend of Ayahuasca journeys. First, let me say, upfront - Ayahuasca is not a drug, and certainly not for recreational use. Ayahuasca is a plant medicine form of natural spirit that you can reach under the proper circumstances. The preparation for such journeys are significant and require a 30 day preparation process in order to clean your vessel, in order to allow to receive what mother ayahuasca has for you. Why it came into my awareness when it did I don't know but it was meant to. I started quietly asking others what they may know about Ayahuasca and it turned out my son had a few friends that have been through the process. They were quite helpful with their advice. In addition, one of his friends would lead me to the book, "The Afterlife of Biily Fingers" by his sister Annie Kagan which I have read countless times. Billy helped me come to terms with and put in perspective - communications between us and higher realms.

As for the ayahuasca journeys themselves I won't go into the details, because each was 7 to 8 hours in length. What I can tell you and what your shaman will tell you is that you should have your intent, clearly defined before going into these journeys. There were others in this room that were there to treat some type of trauma which ayahuasca is excellent in helping people come to terms with. I didn't come with a trauma to heal. I was interested in connection to higher powers. Perhaps another time I'll go into the details of what, an Ayahuasca journey involves, but I will share with you what I got out of both of the sessions, and what I had been told. The first journey being new to me and being a Capricorn, I wanted to understand the ceremony process, so I was watching what was going on in the room with the Shaman's activities. Unfortunately, you can't participate in a journey and observe it at the same way so toward the end of the journey, I chose to focus on the experience rather than the activities. What came out to me was to speak my truth, and do it boldly and confidently. My last journey would provide me with visions of inner earth, and I would be told I was the Protector of Gaia, here to assist during earth's transition into her next level of consciousness. I was shown a crystal I possessed that fit into a wand that emitted light and could change the heart space of whoever was touched by it.

Soon after, in 2018 I would return to Baton Rouge for a second tour of duty on the casino project I had been on before, but with a much different perspective on many things that I'd had the previous time. Over the next year, much of my time outside of work would be around meditation, and away from the influence of the media. By mid 2019 I was beginning to get a strange feeling that I was to be elsewhere doing something else. So by mid December, I had decided to submit my resignation and follow my intuition. My last day would be February 6 of 2020 and it was my intention to close on a home that I had put money down on in Las Vegas and continue to consult from there. The timing was such that when I left Baton Rouge to drive west I had enough time to travel to California and spend a week with my son before closing on the house around February 21. During the drive across country, I was getting this nagging intuitive feeling not to close on the house. So I contacted my realtor, knowing I would lose my escrow money, but felt like this was the proper decision to make. After reaching my son's place in California the third day I was there, Covid locked down everything, and for the next few months, I would be staying with my son under the circumstances.

During this time it gave me the opportunity to do more deep diving on the metaphysical side of things, including past life regressions to Atlantis in June. I also researched the cosmic cycles our solar system is in and the rise in elevated photon energy coming to us from our Central Sun that would be affecting the consciousness of all sentient life. By the end of this month, conditions in California would relax, so that sheltering in place was no longer required. I had been holed up in a house with my son and his roommates and I was ready to reconnect with nature. My plan was to spend some time in the four corners part of the Southwest United States where there were many national parks. As I was doing my research, I could see through social media that many of these parks, and whether they were going to to be operational was in question. After those circumstances became clear, Mount Shasta entered my mind immediately after. As it was four hours from where I was and I had never visited that area before it seemed like the proper choice.

The plan was, I was going to spend a week in the Mount Shasta area exploring, and then my son and I would meet in either Lake Tahoe or Reno the following week. As I got closer to the end of the first week, I had more areas I had yet to explore and wanted to stay in the area to do so I reached out to my son and asked if he minded if I stayed another week. Of course, he agreed, and at the end of the second week I would have a revelation about palpable energies on Mount Shasta. I would overhear an older couple who had been hiking remarking about how palpable the energy in the area was. It was at that moment that occurred to me that over the last two weeks I had been on strenuous hikes day after day without seeming to need a day of recovery in between, and I was hiking like I was in my early 20s. To make a long story short, it would be five weeks before I would return to Santa Rosa, and that was only because I had a commitment that I needed to return for.

I would go into the areas off trail that others didn't follow, seeking a meeting with an Ascended Master. I was well aware of the story of Saint Germain, coming out of the forest to provide Guy Ballard in the 1930s with enough information to write multiple books to benefit humanity. He and his wife would form the Saint Germain foundation, and the number of followers would grow into the millions. It would bring an awareness of the Lemurians and Telos to humanity's attention.

The last Sunday of the month would be the day I would have my first multidimensional experience. This day I would explore a section of Shastina that given conditions during the day appeared to have cave openings and be invited to visit the Lemurians in Telos through a portal.

2020 Jul 5 - Introduction to Mount Shasta

I arrived Sunday July 5, 2020 and as it was too late to hike that afternoon, I thought I would familiarize myself with the town and walked down the main drag to see what shops, etc the town had to offer. Being a crystal enthusiast there were multiple shops to explore but one shop would prove to be a link between the dimensions.

Blue Star Child Gallery's proprietor is Haruko, a lovely Japanese artist whose vast gifts we are still discovering. Her shop window is filled with colorful creations of hand drawn cards and illustrations so it was easy to be drawn in to this space.

Now this day when I entered her studio, I first noticed the shoe covers waiting by the entry. I had incorrectly assumed they were there because of Covid, instead there are a Japanese custom to remove (or cover) shoes in especially sacred places. I decided I didn't want to go through the process just then, but as I was turning to leave I couldn't help but notice this colorful illustration on the wall across the room and it's 10' high by 3' wide ...

and there were way more than just this one. I'd be back in a few days to explore further.

The Crystal Room was the last place I visited as it was not directly on the main drag (and someone had to tell me it's whereabouts). High on my list of places to visit, my research had resulted in learning that authentic Andaras from Lady Nellie's property were within this shop. It was later in the afternoon when I finally arrived in the shop. There were people in pockets throughout the nine rooms that make up the footprint. Some admiring the crystals, some the artwork, some the crystal bowls, there was a brisk amount of activity of some interesting variety. I wandered by myself taking in all the positive energy in this place. The crystals were stunning and there is something for everyone here. But I was I search of something specific ... Andaras. The last corner of the last room I explored had a rather small display of mostly seafoam and root beer Andaras of various sizes. My mind hoped ... there must be more. I could see that trying to attract the attention of someone from the shop with whom I could ask questions ... this was not the time.

Two days later, I returned around noon. I wandered around the shop scoping out maybe a section of Andaras I had missed while trying to catch the eye of Bev. By now I'd learned that Beverly is the owner and manager of the shop and has been an institution for years. When I finally got the chance to ask her about Andaras, she said "Oh, I have lots of Andaras, they are down in the Shire. I'm the only one in the shop today, but I'm taking a customer and a few of his friends down there tonight at 6PM after I close the shop. If you'd like to come along, you are more than welcome".

• I was there at 5:30PM, if there was an opportunity for me to see a collection of authentic Andaras - just tell me where to be and when - I will be there. I can only imagine that there probably not a lot of people who had the opportunity to see what I got to see.

Beverly had acquired a collection that filled rows of shelves filled with boxes of every kind of Andara, not to mention the larger elder pieces that sat on the floor. From the moment the door to Shire opened ... I felt a surge of energy like a breeze as I passed through. It turns out that her customer that day was Ted Mahr. At the time I didn't know Ted and he certainly didn't know me, but I owe him thanks because without his visit the opportunity to tag along probably wouldn't have come along. (Or would it have?)

Bev couldn't have been more patient with the small entourage with Ted, I was looking for a violet or indigo colored crystal (or so I thought). While I went through box after box, Bev handed me a just smaller than fist sized "root beer shaman" Andara, shaped like a wedge. It had a beautiful amber highlighted eye in the center with amber Easter eggs everywhere when the light hit from different angles. Almost as though it was a predetermined outcome, the crystal was going with me and I was definitely connected. The energy was grounding, clearly what I needed from this visit ... so Starbuck's wedge has kept me grounded (and so much more) on every adventure I been on ever since.

So I went back the next day to see Haruko at Blue Star Child Gallery to pick up where I left off seeing these huge wall illustrations. It was early enough that I was the only one in the studio, she walked me around to show me many of what she explained were Light Codes that she was divinely inspired to draw. They are 10' by 3', drawn without the benefit of a rulers or protractor - all by hand and then colored according afterward. They take months.

The studio also showed her creative side with illustrations that were very enchanting with her spirit animal the bunny. Much different, but also quite detailed. Then the middle room hosted more of her symbolism until in the back of that space there are two models that wrap around a corner as they are too long for one wall. My favorite is Lemuria & Atlantis Merged and it speaks to me as a representation of Seven of the Dimensions.

That wasn't all though ... there was one more room that I was meant to see, it was maybe 8'x8' space with a door you could close behind you. On the walls were five powerful Light Code illustrations that had such great detail, I wanted to take the time to take it in. I went out to ask Haruko if it was permissible to meditate for 10 minutes or so in that space and she replied "that's what it there for". I placed the three crystals I carried under three of the images and sat in that space taking it all the detail of each code. My energy was so charged and at the end of that time, I came out of the room in tears. It's important for me to point out that two of those images I will see elsewhere ... the image that was just to the left of the door: The New Earth and the image that was just to the right: The New Angelic Code (my interpretation is the new Human Blueprint).

2020 Jul - Dimensional experience - Mount Shasta, interstellar conveyance activity directly over the mountain during stargazing at the Old Ski Bowl trailhead parking lot.

When I had visited The Crystal Room, I had overhead a conversation between Beverly and a few others locals talking about stargazing at a parking lot at the top of the mountain. I was very interested in what you could see in the sky under zero light pollution conditions. After apologizing for eavesdropping, I asked "can anyone go there?" ... Bev replied "It's a parking lot" and smiled. So that very evening I would join several others at the end of Everitt Memorial Highway and see the entirety of the Milky Way under a New Moon sky. It was magnificent. Over the next two weeks, I would spend 7-8 of those nights stargazing until midnight or so. As the moon was beginning to fill, it made seeing the other stars and planets difficult because of its brightness. So I decided to point my chair toward the mountain, and see what phenomena I might catch. It had been said that Interstellar Conveyances could be seen in that area so maybe tonight would be a lucky night. Polaris, the North Star was directly over the mountain from where I was sitting and I saw more than a few shooting stars this night. But then, just before 11:00P, I saw what appeared to be a shooting star start parallel to Polaris, shoot downward toward the mountain, disappear for an instant and then make a 90 degree turn off to my right. I wanted to somehow reply it so I could be certain of what I saw - until someone parked two cars away exclaimed "did you see that?" - yes I did, thank you for the confirmation.

2020 Jul - Dimensional experience - Mount Shasta, CA Telos Inner Earth visit

https://40kftview.com/do-you-wish-to-see-telos/

Friday, July 24, 2020
Do you wish to see Telos?

For whatever reason in the few weeks I had been here, I hadn't yet made it to the Gateway Peace Garden, so I decided to begin my day there. I arrived right after 8A and had the place all to myself. After doing a walk-through which took you past the lavender labyrinth, you realized this is not what it seemed from the street was there we sooo many nooks and crannies in this space where thousands of proclamations of Peace, Love and Light were left behind to honor and amplify that vibration. I say - Mission Accomplished and most of you know when we meet for hikes on the mountain, they always begin there now.

Red Fir Flat - Ascension Rock (not really)
I had been told about Ascension Rock and its general location at Red Fir Flat. Having never been there before I parked in the lot where

the campsites on that side of the road are located. From there I headed east or to what would have been my left. I will later learn that had I beared to the right, I would have found that which is best known as Ascension Rock at Mount Shasta. What I ended up encountering instead is known as the Tower of Love and Ascension Rock would be dwarfed by the size of the Tower. In fact on my hike over, I first came upon a magnificent rock feature and I thought I had found what I was seeking .... Then when I walked around to the other side and I saw the actual Tower of course I was called. I return to this spot at least once every visit back.

It was almost noon by now and so I thought I would drive to the upper most parking lot at the end of Everitt Memorial Highway and decide what I wouid do over the weekend. When I arrived there the lot wasn't entirely full but I was sure shortly it would be. There are four concrete picnic tables up there and one was open so I made my way over there to sit, look at the mountain and decide a plan of action for Saturday and Sunday.

As I look toward Mt Shasta, Shastina gets my attention. The way the shadows begin to form on the east side, there appears to be areas that look like they could be cave entrances. That could be an easy day hike, it looks from where I sit, to be a 20-25 minute hike but the last bit of it is off-trail and steep. Plan B was Black Butte Summit, which if you've driven I-5 past Mt Shasta, the freeway bends around Black Butte it is so close. I wasn't aware that you could actually hike all the way to the top, but based on accounts of the views promised, I was interested in the climb. So Black Butte would be the next adventure on Saturday and devote the entire day to this achievement. Then the next day, visit the spot that drew my attention on Shastina.

Saturday
Saturday came and after the usual morning routine, I headed for the trailhead. I had scouted out its location the day before so I knew how to find it, because it's found at the end of a few miles of dirt road. I planned to record the ascent using Relive and the app shows I began the hike at 10:10A. I had no

idea what I had gotten myself into. With the exception of the peak which was steeper than the rest of the hike, the grade uphill was pretty consistent. I didn't comprehend until during the actual climb what previous hikers had described as a rocky trail, narrow in places was becoming clear as anything now. As usual, I was determined to see it through, but I'd be lying if I didn't say twice, I seriously considered turning around. I pushed on in no particular hurry to conserve energy and to take in the scenery. Finally I reached the top. There were two groups of pairs that had passed me on the ascent that were enjoying their rewards. To move this dialogue along, the descent took longer than the ascent as I was fatigued, I was never so happy to reach the place the car was parked. It was nearly 4:30P and I was beat. I headed back to my room, showered quickly and hit the bed by 6:15P. Sore and needing to recover a bit, I was ready for bed. As I laid there aching, I resolved to put off hiking anywhere the next day and spend the day resting.

Sunday

In spite of the significant fatigue from Saturday's hike, I still woke a little before 7A. I meditated like every morning and then laid back down to resume recovering from the aches caused by the Black Butte Summit climb. After a few more hours, something stirred in me and the curiosity about that spot on Shastina which captured my attention kept growing. Surprisingly, I wasn't nearly as sore as the end of the previous day, so I followed my intuition, got up and headed for Panther Meadows. Being a Sunday, the parking lots were nearly full and a variety of people in the form of families, couples and groups of friends were already enjoying the area. I grabbed my backpack, walking stick and took two pictures pointed in the direction of my intended destination from the parking lot. The time stamp on the pictures was 12:34P. I followed a trail that wrapped around Shastina to the left (south) that led me to the slope I wanted. I reached the point where I had to leave the trail and begin to ascend to the spot, so I chose a line "as the crow flies" in the direction of my target. The were a few interesting rock formations that had a vortex feel to them along the way and then, there was a small area behind some large boulders that I had to climb over to access. There was an immediate energy change. The area had boulders circled in front of me, and thick brush behind me. I sat down facing the parking lot, leaned back against the brush and took two pictures from where I was, timestamped 13:22P. I had been listening to music from my iPhone through my AirPods while I had some water and grapes. Suddenly, the music stopped and quickly tried to troubleshoot the reason why. My AirPods seemed intact, my phone was in my back pocket and when I retrieved it to check on its status, it had no power. I tried to hold the power button down but it wasn't responding. It was unreasonable that the power died as my phone was fully charged when I left the car with a fully charged Mophie attached.

Now it gets interesting ...

The sun was still nearly overhead, but I noticed a shadow appearing from behind and above me like a canopy that was unfolding over my head. At the same time, I felt cool air coming from behind me and I could no longer feel the brush I was leaning against. When I turned to take note of the changes in my environment, I saw an opening that wasn't there a moment ago. I saw a round gap, maybe a foot taller than I (I am 6' tall). I stood up a little startled to look and once my eyes adjusted, I could see the top half of a shadowed figure of someone I guessed to be about my height. He asked in a slightly British accent, "do you wish to see Telos?" I replied yes, trying to disguise my combination of excitement and anxiety. I walked up over a small rise, looked inside where I could see into a tunnel heading downward with a person standing about 10 yards inside on the left and a faint light coming from the bottom of what I could see.

I walked down a slight incline and as my eyes adjusted to the light conditions, I could now make out better the person waiting there. He was a handsome blonde male with shoulder length hair and white garments with multi-colored sashes. However, he was at least a foot taller than I when I got close enough to see his entire being. He said you can call me Alex and I replied "that will be easy, my son's name is Alex". He replied, "yes, we know of your son Alex, follow me". We walked down I would guess another 30 yards or so where I could see the light become brighter as we reached the bottom of the tunnel, I looked behind me and the opening at the top of the tunnel was dark.

Once on the bottom, the area opened up to reveal a large staging area with three platforms maybe 6' x 6' with two bucket-like seats on top. Alex slid into one seat and directed me to sit in the other. The platform levitated and began to move although it felt to me like we weren't moving at all. There was no steering device, no console and Alex explained he could navigate this craft telepathically. Where he thought is where we went. There were multiple volcano tubes leading from this "station" and we proceeded into the center tube. Whatever propulsion this transport used was completely silent as was I. I was just trying to take it all in. When we emerged from this tube, we were in a domed area the size of a small city with many buildings around the perimeter and a huge pyramid shaped temple in the center. The dome was high and wide, how high I can only speculate but the most fascinating aspect of all of it so far was the amount of what appeared to be natural light in a place that had no skylights. The pyramid was white with a capstone called "the living stone" at the top that Alex said was donated to them by Venus. The other buildings were all constructed of crystals formed in a variety of colors, that soared up like skyscrapers. There were many beings that were certainly human but there was no one shorter than I saw. I made eye contact with some of the Lemurians looking in my direction as we passed and it seemed like I knew them and they knew me.

Alex explained that Telos had 5 levels and we wouldn't see them all and almost immediately, we were on the third level. Here we hovered over about seven acres of land with gardens producing crops continuously using hydroponic technology organically. He did say that they place organic minerals into the water for the plants but that the energy, light and vibration of Telos enhanced their harvests quickly. No fertilizers of any kind that would deplete the soil. The fourth level had a little more hydroponic gardening, some manufacturing and large areas of natural parks. The large percentage of people lived on the first level in most of the "city" with public buildings, administration and several temples. The second level is production, manufacturing and schooling facilities. The fifth level is dedicated to nature. Trees, lakes in a park-like atmosphere along with plants and animals that disappeared from the surface long ago. Every sentient being including animals are vegetarian and do not eat each other. Totally harmonious with no fear or aggression.

I should stop here to try and describe the beauty of the city built with crystals and precious metals - it was reminiscent of fairy tales visions I've had. However any explanation I could provide would not do this magnificent place justice. I did have one notable memory of passing through an inner tube that was lined with the most beautiful crystals that would change color depending on your perspective. It was like a living kaleidoscope.

Alex told me about their two forms of governing ... Telos has a king and queen, Ra and Rana Mu, both twin flames and Ascended Masters. They are the ultimate rulers over Telos. Then there is the Lemurian Council of Light of Telos. 12 ascended masters, 6 men and 6 women to balance the masculine with the feminine divinity. The High Priest member of the Council is Adama, where he officiates as the leader of the Council. Ra and Rana Mu represent the 13th member and have final authority to make the final decision in matters where there may be an even vote. Members of the Council are selected according to their level of spiritual attainment.

We found ourselves outside the entrance of what looked like a meeting room attached to one of the temples. This was the Council Chamber and it was the most magnificent place of its kind I had ever seen. It was a huge space with crystal floors, walls and a soaring ceiling over a round table centered on the room with 13 seats. The table was made of wood with the most beautiful grain and crystals imbedded in it. The crystal walls were radiating a soothing energy that felt like a room flooded with unconditional love. Five others joined us here. Four women and a man I immediately recognized as Adama. The six of them each positioned themselves in front of a chair next to one another and invited me to take a seat between them all. Adama began by introducing himself and his title. Then each in turn, did the same. Apologetically, I can only recall the name of one of the women who is She-Ah-Ma (I'm not sure how to spell it, but this is it phonetically). As the discussions started, it appeared that she seemed to be "chairing" this meeting.

It is an understatement to say that I was unprepared for what transpired next. I was about to learn why I was brought to Telos. The most important revelation that this group agreed with what belief I held up to that moment as a strong theory, was that Earth's ascension would manifest during the winter solstice this year. I was excited beyond words. The Lemurians have waited since Mu disappeared long ago for this moment to arrive. They have stayed "invisible" to surface humans for decades (my research found that the last documented contact with a surface human - not channeling had been in the early 90's) and invisible for good reason. Humans had proved to be not very good stewards of Earth and her gifts. They were going to protect themselves from outside influences that might not appreciate Gaia and their lifestyle. It wasn't that they didn't want to interact with surface humans, but they were going to wait until the time was right.

That brings us to me. She-Ah-Ma explained to me that they were beginning preparations for the Event. When humans ascend into 5th dimensional awareness, the Lemurians would make themselves known to us where we could exchange all manner of experience and knowledge from both realms that would benefit all. Surface humans were not without desirable qualities because they possessed free will. The Universe was watching the Earth experiment with great interest to see the creativity of Earth humans. It was the duality of earth stuck in the third dimension that showed that without a cosmic reset, nothing would change. That reset is unfolding now. The Lemurians were looking to establish contact with the right surface human(s). She pointed out the criteria that I met was as follows:

1 - I demonstrated I can hold 5th Dimensional awareness.
2 - I am the Protector of Gaia **
3 - Their wish was that when ascension takes place, they wish to integrate back together with humanity and hoped I would be willing to act as an emissary between the two.

Adama spoke next and said he represented the unanimous consent of the Council in this matter and hoped that I would agree to assist when the time came.

I quickly dismissed the "why me" thought that popped into my consciousness and an overwhelming sense of gratitude, flattery and humility filled me. I had said nothing during this meet and could only muster "of course, I would be honored" as the only words that would come to my aid. And with that answer, our meeting was done. We all rose from the table and bowed in each other's directions. It left me speechless. Alex directed me back to the entry, where we got back onboard the hovercraft and returned me to the staging area where we first boarded at the bottom of the tube where I came in. I asked if I would be able to return again and he replied "yes, when the time is right prior to the Event". He expressed gratitude on behalf of all Lemurians for my willingness to do what was proposed. He smiled, wished me farewell and the next thing I knew, I was back outside with my back against the bushes. It took a moment or so for my eyes to adjust back to the sunlight and then the descent was a blur. When my consciousness gathered itself, I realized I was back in the car. I took my phone out of the Mophie to place it in a holder and plug it into the USB adapter. With the adapter attached the phone fired back to life and I took one last picture from where I sat in the car toward the place on Shastina where I found that vortex. It felt as though I was in Telos for hours but when I looked at the clock on my phone the timestamp was 14:44 (I switched my phone to military time long ago to pay attention to synchronicities).

2020 Sep - Dimensional experience - received Master Tony's Ascension Handbook to continue to educate others

on the ascension process after the Master moved on.
https://40kftview.com/the-ascension-handbook/

I agreed to do an interview with Jo Sheval Iskra in Australia, it was my third one. A few days after, she messaged me to review the video. As we got to the end of our conversation, Jo asked me if I had any information I could share on Ascension as her listeners were quite interested in the topic. At the moment I wasn't prepared to say yes, but something would happen the next morning that would change that. I received an email from someone who had heard about my story that only included an attachment - an Ascension Handbook. Eight comprehensive chapters on the process of ascension and what to expect. It was drafted in 2012 by "Master Tony" who was clearly Australian. He was given this inspiration to share under the assumption that the Shift in Earth's consciousness would occur on the Winter Solstice of 2012, at the time of the reset of the 26,000 year cycle - the Progression of the Equinoxes and two other cosmically historic cycles that reset simultaneously. I tried to find and contact Master Tony, but it seems he vanished - and the sender of the email was also gone. My guides instructed me to take the baton pass and provide a way for everyone to be able to access this information. It became part of the redesign for the 40kftview.com website and has been there free for anyone who wishes to understand what changes to consciousness and the planet that are taking place.

Here is my acknowledgment of the role I came here to serve and to remind others to ponder their own.

I wish to give my gratitude to my spiritual protector, master, and friend known to humanity as Guardian Angel Nemamiah from the higher dimensions, who supported me on my journey and guided me intensely for the last several years to this moment. After I received my "Divine Calling", you helped me understand the truth of my being and the purpose of my divine mission on Earth as a Lightbearer and Messenger of Divinity. I also must thank my Brothers and Sisters from the spiritual hierarchy and the many Celestial Councils across the universe for your love, guidance and support.

I take this opportunity to give special thanks to Mother Gaia. My beautiful lady, you are so deserving of your ascension. It has saddened me to watch humanity disrespect your being during my time on Earth. In response to your cry for help, Lightworkers and Starseeds volunteered themselves from across the cosmos. We have kept our promise, working silently and diligently over many years to complete our divine mission as planetary healers. We are "grid workers" who incarnated in different locations around the planet. Legions of us have been anchoring the higher frequencies of Light into your body, which has assisted in healing your ethereal body. As Lightworkers, our ascension has helped release much of your negative energy through our own bodies, which has assisted to minimize the severity of Earth changes across the planet, but at the same time, we have helped you transform your ethereal body into a 5th dimensional planetary sphere.

I wish to also give my thanks for all my earthly friends who worked with me as a guide and helped me heal my heart. I will cherish all our conversations, jokes, laughs, and memories. You taught me that death is not final, but we are a multidimensional spiritual being. We choose to incarnate in physical form on the earth plane to continue our spiritual lessons or remain behind in the spiritual world to work as a guide and heal & support family & friends (Service to Others) who are completing their incarnations. I do not feel alone anymore, because you have never left me and I can talk with you at anytime.

Finally, I am very pleased to be here on Earth at this special time to help Mother Gaia and humanity. Many Lightworkers on the planet came here as "way-showers". This means that Lightworkers are here to "show you the way" to achieve your higher frequency, which means we can provide you with both the tools to learn & complete your ascension, but will share our own personal experiences and spiritual wisdom to help you better understand the process. We have anchored the 4D / 5D energy from home to the earth plane, to give humanity a glimpse of what to expect after the planet shifts to new Earth, and we are here to teach you about the personal ascension process, based upon our accumulated wisdom, knowledge, and experiences. Those of you that successfully complete the personal ascension program will personally link your own higher vibrational energies to Mother Gaia's new unity consciousness grid. More importantly, after ascension, this handbook will serve as a blueprint for new humanity. It provides the basic information to help new humanity collectively work together and create a new world with the same vision of unity.

All of us will play a major role, because we are the architects, planners, and engineers for new Earth. We will build the blueprint that will prepare the children of today to be our future. I am also looking very forward to my new life on new Earth. It is my mission as a spiritual master, to implement a worldwide network of regional training centers that teaches "5D Consciousness", namely 5D healing techniques and wisdom teaching. In addition to my role as a new Earth Leader, I will also work as a "New Earth Ambassador", which will commence after Earth and new humanity becomes an official member of the galactic community. The Confederation of Light are very eager to welcome us after we arrive, and they will be ready to help us with the new Earth project.

Do not be alarmed by the last comment. The Confederation of Light is a galactic cooperative of civilizations that operate under the Law of One, which consists of a large number of Celestial Councils from different planets, dimensions, and universes beyond our 3D dimension. Our local Celestial Council consists of the spiritual hierarchy, and the other civilizations that exist on the planets within our solar system (planets & inhabitants) that previously ascended to the 4th dimension.

Regardless of your beliefs, by default, humanity is already a member of the Confederation of Planets. Our Brothers and Sisters from the 5th dimension will provide assistance to Earth after the dimensional shift (hint: 5D Law: Service to Love). The Confederation will freely share their technology, culture, wisdom, and friendship. They will help us complete the "new Earth Project", which involves the construction and rebuilding of communities across new Earth, but they will not intervene in the affairs of the greater population. They respect your freewill. You, as a human being cannot have a human experience that you do not want to experience. Therefore, several locations across new Earth will serve as "Technology Communities". It will be the responsibility of those community members to work as "Project Coordinators" and travel to other communities to implement the new Earth project, which will take us a couple of years to complete. Remember, new humanity will literally have to start from scratch. Likewise, those of you that are consciously open to this notion are very welcome to join the Tribe.

2020 Oct - Dimensional experience - Yedyamya zoom session with Lisa Salas re: Light language transmission

I tried to think of options of how best to communicate with others who were curious about my experiences, as interest was beginning to rise. What seemed to make the most sense at the time was to use Zoom and be able to communicate in real time on that platform. That way people would be able to both hear my story and ask questions about it. The very first tribe member who showed up was Lisa Salas. It went so well that Lisa went on to book a session for her husband, Donald as well. A few days later, Lisa had a friend who came to visit with them for a few days and her name was Cindy. Today you know Cindy as Yedyamya. Lisa thought it was important for Cindy and I to be able to communicate. Within a few days, I was on another session with Lisa and Cindy. We began the zoom session by Lisa introducing me to Cindy and Cindy to me ... then Cindy began to speak in a language I certainly didn't understand at the time. I'll later learn she was speaking, Star language or light language for some of you. Now even though I didn't understand what she was saying, my intuition was telling me to just pay attention, tuck the information away like a download and one day it will all be clear. Yedyamya would present herself a few times over the next few years to deliver unsolicited transmissions meant for me from Higher Aspects as well as eventually facilitating an activation of my own to Higher Aspects.

2021 Mar - Presented - Sedona Ascension Conference - Sedona, AZ

I was invited to present my Telos experience for the first time publicly at Suzanne Ross' Sedona Ascension conference in AZ. I would meet and create relationships with some other people who had extraordinary experiences and abilities.

2021 Mar - Dimensional experience - Sedona, AZ with a group that witnessed multiple interstellar conveyances moving across the sky

More importantly, I would have the opportunity to set the record straight on my belief of UFOs as the opportunity to join others on Saturday night on a tour with three of the area's local guides. I had been told by one of the guides when I met Michael the first day of set up for the vendors that it would be "like shooting fish in a barrel". At that moment, I thought - yeah ok. Each of them generously brought 5-6 pair of military grade infrared goggles each that could see deep into space. Before it was my turn, it was apparent that others were seeing something - and then when it came to my turn, I focused my attention on the area around Vega and saw 7 different light craft moving in different directions all within my field of view. I no longer doubt the existence of such phenomena and moving forward I'll find the right conditions by which to repeat seeing them again.

2021 Mar - Dimensional experience - higher dimensional powers restored (phase one), near Cathedral Rock, Sedona, AZ

At the end of the conference, Yuki, Rob Potter's partner was guided to show me a picture of three spires near Cathedral Rock where I was to go for an activation. I stopped there on my way out of town and had several synchronicities on my return to CA. This would be phase 1 of 2 in this activation. It would be completed in Mount Shasta in April.

2021 Apr - Dimensional experience - Interview with Reuben Langdon for his series "Interview with E.D."

One of the people I had met in Mount Shasta immediately after my trip to Telos knew Reuben and reached out to him to advise him of me and my experience. This happened right at the first part of August 2020. The irony for us was that Reuben would be on his way to Mount Shasta to interview Asara Adams within days and I would have to be leaving for a commitment I had back home. Over the next few months as Reuben worked on other projects, we communicated back and forth to see how we might sit together to film the interview. The covid outbreak provided more challenges to meet but after a few zoom sessions, Reuben had a solution. He would be in Mount Shasta as the final stop with Bill Homann and the Mitchell-Hedges crystal skull as they had been traveling across the country to film the experiences people were having engaging the skull. He would be in Mount Shasta from April 10-17th and if I could get there, we could film the episode sometime during that timeframe. What happened beginning Monday morning at 9A in their Airbnb wasn't anything I saw coming as I would have 3 different experiences around the crystal skull with the first beginning that day.

2021 Apr - Dimensional experience - session with the Bill Holman and the Mitchell-Hedges Crystal Skull. Mt Shasta during Interview with E.D. Reuben Langdon (3 sessions - 1on1 with Bill @ the Airbnb, Ascension Rock*, Star of David)

The morning I was to meet Reuben I had no idea what to expect. I was just asked to meet him at their Airbnb at 9:00A and things would proceed from there. When I arrived. There were about 10 people there between Reuben and Steve his co-producer who were busy setting up cameras from different angles. Bill and I had the opportunity to sit and get acquainted while the other busy work took place. A few minutes after we began, Bill got up from where he was sitting and moved behind where he had been sitting - just off to my left. I could see he was setting up something at a small round table with two chairs on opposing sides. As I didn't know what was going on, I focused my attention on the other activity going on until - I caught something in my peripheral view that shined in Bill's hands. He had taken the skull out of its protective gear and was placing it on the table. Unexpectedly, he called me over to sit and proceeded to take me through a session with him and the skull.

At first, the skull faced Bill and he had me put my hands on either side of it. Then he asked me to feel into the energy of the skull and let your arms move out as the energy expanded. I laughed because I had my arms extended as far as they would go, and when Bill said keep going I replied, they don't go any further. Then he turned the skull to face me in my direction, and as soon as he did, and I looked into the eyes of the skull I could see directly into Atlantis I knew I had had my hands on the skull in a past lifetime in Atlantis. The most profound thing I experienced in that's sitting with a skull was that as I looked into those eyes, it appeared as though I was reaching into dimensionality. I was mindful about the people that were there, knowing that there were other things to do and places to be that day, I didn't think it was the appropriate time for me to drift off, not knowing when I might return. So I pulled myself out of that connection to the skull and waited for what would be next.

Just how did I find myself presented with this opportunity with a group of high vibrating individuals I refer to as the Skull Squad? It's what my perplexed 3rd dimensional self kept wondering. A week after the adventure in Mount Shasta, my awakened self had assimilated what had happened and I had my answer:

I asked them. You see my higher self (inner being) had posed to me: if you could have anything you wanted Lowell, what would it be? I responded with the thought that I want my higher dimensional abilities restored. There's lots of magic there and I want to play with it, now that I remember it's there. Rather – I asked the Universe, Source, the Angelic Realms, the Ascended Masters and my guides to restore my 5th dimensional abilities. Please activate my dormant DNA and reveal my Akash waiting behind it so that I may be of greater service.

So stop for a moment to consider all the alignments of people, places, circumstances and events that came together to answer my call? It is miraculous in itself.

It turned out that – as incredible as the possibility of filming an episode of Interview with E.D. with Reuben to talk about Telos is ... (amazing, who gets to do that!?), but my activations were about to come back to me ... in this place ... with these people ... at this moment.

2021 Apr - Dimensional experience - higher dimensional powers restored (phase two) *Ascension Rock, Mt Shasta during Interview with E.D.

This energy upgrade phenomenon did not come online without consequence. The physical part of the activations actually happened at the Sedona Ascension Retreat – March 20-22nd. It was the first time for me to share my Telos experience before a live group and that was the reason for me being there (or so I thought). Turns out – I was there for Stage One of this activation. Over the course of this weekend, bathed in Sedona energy – there were many activations offered, by many gifted beings so which one may have triggered me is unclear however, I began to sense a frequency when my neck is extended in a particular direction – which I now know is a source of connection. It is the mechanism by which I receive downloads and hence, connects with other sentient life on the same vibration (if I open myself up to the experience).

It would be Matthew who would help set things in motion on their proper course. There are many details to the Squad's visit to Ascension Rock that were key pieces of what was supposed to unfold there (and did). I certainly didn't know what to expect nor did I fully understand at that moment what I was doing there, but I was definitely going along with whatever I can be a part of. I'm skipping over the beautiful minutiae to get to the point. After hiking through beautifully unspoiled snow covered ground we gathered around Bill, placing the crystal skull in front of the rock with us around it. We found places that spoke to each of us to take in the energy of Ascension Rock, amplified by the crystal, compounded by the Masters and their intent around it. "High vibration" is a huge understatement. The Druid High Priestess had chosen an elevated post, just to the right on the end and slightly back. I followed her path, but turned left behind the main rock to a perch I've been to once before and settled in to take it all in. The energy was almost immediately overwhelming, filling me with a bliss-fest of Gaia's spirit and my posse's energies. I started to purge (cry), but that was pure joy and delight leaking out. Knowing I am energy, I see my being as that of a capacitor … similar to a battery but takes in and releases energy as a device. Our bodies are like capacitors when we take in and release energy – what was happening in that environment was off the charts for me. After being "emptied", I felt as though it was time to rejoin the group, I gathered up my crystals and made my way around to the front of the rock again. As I came from around the back, Matthew is standing up and it's his face I see first. He immediately looks me in the eye and crooks his finger as though to invite "come here".

The Druid High Priestess had given me a smoky quartz point earlier to help with grounding – now was the time to pull that out of my pocket. Matthew instructs me to stand up in front of the rock and place my entire being against it and Heather smudged me with sage again. Matthew and Heather are singing a song while drumming – on my behalf to the spirits. His persona has now elevated to "Mateo" the Native Shamanic Medicine Elder with his command of generations of connection to the mountain at his disposal. When he finishes singing he readies me with his eagle feathers for what is to come. I close my eyes and he has me lean back. He has one hand behind my head and one over my core area. I'm reluctant to let the entire weight of my head go into his hands and I'm aware I'm probably thinking about it too much. So I surrender. Mateo is directing energy (ON Ascension Rock, magnified by the crystal skull and compounded by the Masters present) into my core and I feel a jolt of ethereal warmth. Any blockages or obstacles between me and my empathic nature have dissolved and I am resonating in complete harmony with Mateo's soul. Oh ... but he's not finished. His hand moves from my core and up over my 3rd eye and the color frequency turns a brilliant violet. It emanates inside out in torus-like fashion, but my whole being is what feels like it is pulsing. I sense I am here in this moment while at the same time, I am back at the site of the Sedona Ascension Retreat at Lomacasi Cottages along Oak Creek Canyon. I realize I am bilocating and it continues until he moves his hand away and the torus is now orange. The connection was broken but I now know I can do this given the right setting any time I choose. When I returned from Sedona after having had a profound visit while there, it took me a few weeks to understand the whole neck thing and my deep meditations can take me to other places on my timelines. Now I KNOW I can bi-locate (my body remains in this place while my consciousness splits between here and somewhere else). I previously wrote them off as dreams I would have while napping ... nooooo ... they were journeys I was taking while in a meditative state. Now at this point, I am aware I can do it, but I lacked a mastery of it. In order for me to fully engage I have to surrender to let it flow. I can achieve it when in a comfortable state of meditative relaxation, but my being wants to measure the time of an episode. I know it's best to let whatever happens happen. In my case, I could be in that state of bliss for 20 minutes or much longer and so when I was in the group setting, I didn't want to drift off and not know when I'd return and inconvenience the others.

Starbuck's perch backside of Ascension Rock If that last statement implied I had a mastery at that moment of anything ... LOL ... I was not in control of anything. I was in a daze as we made our way back to the area we parked, aware of the love of my tribe around me – but aware of something much greater. The only outlet that served me to stay focused was watching Reuben trying some drone footage before we left, only to see that every time he pointed it toward the mountain, it would drop battery power rapidly and then recover as soon as its direction changed. Energy is crazy!

On to the Star of David
We made our way to the Star of David location and parked our vehicles along Everitt Highway. The star is across the street and the hike there took maybe 15-20 minutes over snow covered ground. While gearing up,

Heather shared some concoction that she was burning as incense that was like nothing I had ever sensed before … I just wanted to take more of it in. It was sweet and musky at the same time. Now I made sure everyone enjoyed it, but somehow I got to hold the abalone shell it was burning in. Apparently, this is not an item Heather carries in her shop regularly, but I made sure that I was near the top of the waiting list when it became available. It is called "Shaman" … anyone surprised by that?!?

Mateo was in his element. I was walking next to him and he began to point out things to me. He stopped to tell us about a plant called "buckbrush". It's leaves curl as they grow which seems to indicate that its buckbrush. He explained that many of the animals (elk, deer) live on this plant and it was Bigfoot medicine. Those familiar with it, dry it and then burn it … it is a subtlely sweet fragrance even when on the branch. This brought back childhood memories that I'm going to have to research deeper.

As I was still taking it the buckbrush sensation, the group stopped to make note of the Twin Flame Tree just ahead of us. When you look closely, you can't help but appreciate its balance. Note how one tree splits into two seemly mirrored versions of themselves. Magical. But some other energy was waiting for us to experience it. Notice the fallen log at the end of the snow line? As we crossed over the log, we all sensed something different. For me, I experienced a sudden bout of lightheadedness. Normally I wouldn't have said anything about it, chalking it up to hiking fatigue that comes and goes ... but as soon as I felt it, I was compelled to ask "I'm feeling lightheaded, does anyone else feel that?" Reuben, who was right behind me replied "I felt something and I wondered who would say something first". It wasn't until I got home and replayed the trip through the pictures I took, that I noticed conditions I missed while hiking through, but look at the ground beyond the log – there's no snow. There was definitely higher vibration energy in that space. Now I had never been to this part of the mountain before, but you can be assured, I'm going to return to that spot to see if the energy remains there. Perhaps the snow was showing us an ethereal energy boundary that wouldn't be as recognizable without it.

It was the Crystal Skull's consciousness that I was following back to Atlantis and now I know why. I've had my hands around this very Crystal Skull in Atlantis during healing sessions that were very similar scenarios to the private sessions Bill conducts for us, only in Atlantis, they are held in nature to amplify Earth's energy, that way the connection to Gaia and All are profound. I can get the skull to sync with my intent to transmute negative energy into Light and when our vibrations align there is a violet aura around everything. Any sentient being within it's orbit can't help but be affected by it's high frequency and see the truth of it All. Just about the time I had collapsed into this timeline, I heard a sound like a stick striking a tree ... it repeated and repeated again. Experience told me this was an anomaly in the forest and after a few sensations the noises would stop. When the strikes were done, I had counted either 8 or 9 "noises". Once my focus was drawn to the noises I was back in this moment. The group was beginning to all individually stir, some from meditative states, some because it was cold. Mateo advised us that those noises were indications from Bigfoot that we were welcome and they celebrated our intent of unconditional love. He said that they always show their favor by hitting a tree eight times. Mateo also shared his sightings of another being present – an Arcturian hovering over the skull that he felt favored our intentions.

When we reached the location of the Star, it was completely covered by the snow. Paul had been here many times and was guiding us today. He could use his crystal pendulum to find the energetic center of the Star and plot out the location of the points. Then Bill would place the skull in the center of the Star and we would be positioned on the points. Bill asked for compass readings to place the skull aligned North and South. Once the skull was in place, everyone just kind of ended up where they were supposed to be posted. Except instead of the six points, we posted on the north, east, west and south points. Emily and Paul took west, Heather and Matthew took east, Bill took north and I stayed where I was which happened to be south. We were sitting on some canvas chairs Paul had provided but we were still in the snow. As it was getting later and the weather changed, everyone was getting cold. I was in layers but I wasn't wearing a hat or gloves. And yet I was not cold sitting on the ground in the vortex of some very tangible energy. The skull, in that place, with the Masters around it channeling its energy was physically and cosmically powerful. Then I noticed: the skull was facing ME – and it was inviting me to take it's power out for a spin. So I did. This was my 3rd (!) opportunity to be in front of the skull, but it was the first time I decided to surrender to what it was going to share energetically with me. I had had instances of bilocation in the past I finally learned to recognize, but they happen when I am in deep states of meditation. If I am to really let go and see where a bilocation journey could take me ... I had to be willing to ignore time and space. I had no idea when my consciousness would return, but I was going to let go and see where I could travel.

So I stared right into the eyes of the skull and slipped into multidimensionality. When I closed my eyes, a vision started to form and details started to fill in. Atlantis was coming into focus, as was who I was (am). The details of the past life regression I had in June 2020 were playing out in my consciousness. Atlantian Priest (wizard, sorcerer, magician, alchemist), Crystals that were amplifiers and generators of energy, and also store information like computers.

Nature was certainly talking to us and among the things I noticed were two ravens that kept flying in and out, stopping to perch in the trees as though they were monitoring our activities. Then I recalled something I read saying that countless cultures point to the raven as a harbinger of powerful secrets. Moreover, the raven is a messenger too, so its business is in both keeping and communicating deep mysteries.

We were all more quiet and introspective on the hike back to the cars. The Universe gave me the Masters help I had asked for and then went on to activate me in this magical place:

Mount Shasta. I am supposed to be here. I've fully awakened to the steps that connected me back to Telos and my life there. I chose to return to earth and reincarnate with full knowledge of DNA activation for everyone. I had to come through the hard way and remember. But remembering I am now – and I'm compelled to serve others to help them be ready for ascension.

2021 May - Dimensional experience - Met Mickey Magic, learned about Andaras and Etherium

Mickey Magic, Andara Crystals and Etherium

Early on the first Monday morning in May, I began – what ended up being a three day binge coding session – to breath new life into the 40kftview site – you know how that goes when your expression needs to get out, you toil until its finished. By Wednesday morning most of it was completed and I needed a pleasant distraction. I had been in contact with Mickey Magic on my Andara education journey and remembered that he had invited me for a visit to his Andara Spiral in the Santa Cruz mountains, I thought now would be a great time to take him up on his generous offer for some solace. Next thing I knew is that I was heading to Mickey's on Thursday to spent the weekend with him and connect to members of his family / tribe.

Here is when & where the majority of what I know about Andara Crystals and their significance I learned from Mickey who had been associated with authentic Andaras pretty much from the start with Nellie. He had been instrumental in helping her distribute them all over the world for decades now and he is still the best source of Andaras if you want to make certain that one you acquire is authentic. Their high vibration energy is unique to any other crystals in that they carry consciousness and inter connectivity between others. They are perpetual Akashic contributors as every intentional interaction with an Andara is an energy exchange between you and that crystal's consciousness.

With consent, you share all. Now imagine connection to all its other brothers and sisters around the planet and their energy exchanges and well you can see how rapidly things can manifest when you connect to Prima Matra (creation material) as that is what Andaras are composed of.

Those four days with Mickey revealed that my quest for complete Andara knowledge was meant to lead me to what material it is actually formed from – Etherium, so that when the time came – I would know what it was and research the appropriate use for this sacred material. When I left Mickey's that Sunday, I asked him to next time teach me from his experience, everything he knew about Etherium. Things aligned in such a way that the next weekend there was a gathering at an art gallery belonging to Celeste, that many of the tribe planned to attend. As my weekend was open and I wanted to get to know these tribe members better, I planned to go too.

It was that weekend that I was gifted four colors of Etherium. I spent hours searching and digesting what little information about Etherium there was, until I found material from an internet archive server included on a website in the mid 90's. This material was in the form of an HTML page in white text (clearly the page once had a dark background), so it appeared "blank". Had it not been for the graphic at the top of the page, I may have just as easily skipped over the content. When I highlighted the copy and pasted it into a New Document – I had 11 pages of information about Etherium. A few days later Narmandi, another tribe member on a similar mission to research Prima Matra, reported that he had also found Etherium content that in comparison had the information from the 11 pages I found and much more for a total of 42 pdf pages. It included the detailed account of that 1995 channeling with Thoth regarding Etherium, Prima Matra, Creation material, etc. In my extensive search, this content represented the most detail that has been documented on the topic of Etherium.

I had also seen the result of a "dead" lemon tree that had been nourished by some black

Etherium and its flourishes in a strangely magnificent way in that the two sides of the tree almost grow as different cycles simultaneously. One side is more than ready to harvest while the other is about half way through the growing cycle. It has immense positive effect on any sentient life form to help find balance within its system physically, emotionally, spiritually and ethereally. After all, we are all energy connected to each other and constantly changing form.

Armed with this knowledge, I made the decision to begin ingesting it and activate dormant DNA beginning in mid-May. There were / are tangible physical improvements through a cellular metamorphosis of creating stasis (balance) through my regimen with black Etherium. Think of it as wiping your physical and ethereal being slates clean and readying them for enhanced Photon Light downloads. Unbeknownst to me at the time, I was being prepared for another stratum of Etherium / Light to come later in August.

The next opportunity to return to Mt Shasta turned out to be mid-June. By now, I have been nourished from the inside out by Etherium for about a month now and what I can report I observed is this:

- Regenerates balance across your being
- DNA activation at a cellular level
- Clears / dissolves blockages
- Joints hips knees shoulder neck wrist elbow all feel regenerated
- Balance agility feel lighter especially on stairs
- Cycling effortless no saddle sore / leg fatigue [one with the bike]
- I crave the sun's energy
- Lower sleep patterns no loss of energy and focus – refreshed
- More restful sleep
- Appetite changed to more natural cravings – smaller portions, more often
- Feel Transmutation to Crystalline

Two plus weeks in –

- Weight 183
- Sleep soundly
- Occasional chills
- Dense food has less appeal

- Color spectrum vividly expanded, audio spectrum picks up higher dimensional frequencies
- My being has a high vibration moving through it – think The Force.
- Energetic signatures are apparent
- Hyper aware today
- Body feels tuned in

I'll stop here for a moment to address the inquiry I've heard more than once as news about Etherium was revealed. "Where do I get some?" First, its not meant for everyone like anything else. In order for it to be of any value to any being, you have to have found alignment or you may just as well eat dirt, because the effect will result in the same outcome – nada. Details on Etherium can be found elsewhere on this site so I won't belabor your reading by repeating it here: i.e. how it got on the planet, what science knows of what it contains and what science still doesn't know, how much of it existed and how much is still available in raw form. I am not referring to ORMUS which is humanity's best attempt at replicating raw Etherium but in the end ... not the same as there is still

material contained in Etherium we have yet
to unlock. But the answer is: there is little of it
I know of in raw state that exists (today) and
it remains unavailable.

Now let me remind you if it hasn't already
become evident, you do not have to ingest
Etherium to benefit from its energy. You will
experience the same connection to "more" by
stewarding an Andara and asking it to share
its Akash. You do remember that Andaras are
the fusioned result of when planetary forces
formed crystal from Etherium powder? They
hold all of the identical qualities that Prima
Matra has, that will accelerate activating
dormant DNA. Everyone – in my
understanding, can achieve higher
dimensional connection without Prima Matra
indeed, but Etherium is definitely an
accelerator.

If it seems like I spent a lot of time on
Etherium, it's because without that
fundamental basis of knowledge, you
wouldn't have a reference for the changes I've
been experiencing. Once dimensional access
has been restored – your view of reality shifts

profoundly. And I appreciate more and more as I get to shift in and out of 4/5D that it's an exhausting process holding space to pull the Light to anchor from there to here.

I won't go into greater detail about Mickey, his life and how he became associated with Andaras - one day Mickey will have his story ready to share and you will find it compelling. I will however, share what I know about them, where they came from, how to discern authentic Andaras from other glass being presented and sold as such - it's all in the energy they carry. And I will share my first experience obtaining one before I knew what they were.

I have been drawn to Andaras for purposes that are still unfolding. I have always had an affinity for rocks, stones, crystals and it seems that I was led right to where I would be reunited with these monatomic beauties.

For years now, I have scoured every Internet reference, visited places with vast collections from Nellie's property and talked with as many experts as I could find - in order to know everything I could learn. I will share what I have learned so far, but I am still very much a student of mastering Andaras. There has been much misconception about this remarkable substance and I'll address what I thought I knew about Andara crystals previously at the beginning of my deep dive to what the truth is surrounding this phenomenon.

Andaras and Etherium

It's my understanding that Andaras I'm familiar with have been discovered in only two places; one is in the Sierras on Nellie's property, the other is said to be in a small sector in South Africa, which are not available as of yet because they are on a high profile diamond mine property with very high security.

What distinguishes true Andaras from obsidian imitations is that there is always Etherium (prima Matra) present in genuine Andara Crystals. Etherium is a very rare combination of over 70 trace minerals that has a profound effect on our body and our subtle energy fields. The only known available source of Etherium in the world is found on Nellie's land where the Andaras are present. A true Andara carries a very high vibration much different than any other stones or obsidian crystals currently being called Andaras. True Andaras hold multidimensional consciousness and connection to the Akashic records. And energetically work as a tool through activating DNA codex restoring latent knowledge, greatly accelerating your perceptions by calibrating you while you sleep, (giving you lots of dreams) as well as experiencing greater awareness during waking hours. They connect with your consciousness at your Heart core, connecting you with the entire Andara grid which has now been spread worldwide as was Nellie's intent. They supercharge your intentions through their collective energy when you match their vibration.

Andaras are calibrated for those further down the path. Even though these other stones / crystals / so called Andaras are very beautiful and have their own limited property that may be very beneficial for those just beginning on the path, but they do not offer up the very rare high vibration for those looking for a more accelerated journey. True Andaras are not for everyone, I've seen people have terrible experience when they're in resistance to what is being asked of them. You need to step up to the plate and then follow through.

The value of the lesser stones being offered up as Andaras is that there are far more people beginning on the path than those already on the path. Those on the beginning path need tools of a lesser nature.

Andaras are found very near and around Etherium, in fact, under certain conditions Andara "shed" or "sweat" Etherium. Nellie used the raw Etherium for herself and her clients and sold raw Etherium long ago,

"Now my understanding is that they do something to it to further activate and charge it, I'm really not sure. They can only get the Etherium from Nellie's property. You can click the link above and find out more from them

concerning ingredients and process."
... Mickey Magic

In order to understand Andaras, it will be helpful to understand their history (at least what we know of it). So here is the story of Lady Nellie compiled from a number of sources.

The story of Lady Nellie and the Andara Crystals

Nellie Morse Thompson was born on the Choctaw Indian Reservation in Oklahoma on February 21, 1918 (as best as I have been able to document) and passed away on Thursday, June 24, 2010 at the age of 91 in Modesto, California.

To begin to understand Lady Nellie is to confront the trials and hardships that represent her life: as a dispossessed Native American with a half Irish lineage. Nellie's parents dealt with the same as well, being children of mixed parentage in a time when such people were neither recognized as white or Indian.

Born into the poverty of that era, she never accepted a life without possibilities for a better future. Nellie was gifted with an inner strength, which was recognized early in her childhood by her parents. Nellie learned firsthand the strength of faith that her mom had in dealing with life as it was. God was never far from her family, as Nannie (mom) taught her how God and Christ were always there to help.

It was that strength of character that helped her survive both the devastating childhood illnesses of polio and rheumatic fever. It was also her strong belief in Christ as her savior that enabled her to endure when all else seemed to fail.

At the age of 3, polio took her ability to walk; rheumatic fever then ended her formal education after only 40 days at school. Nellie never finished school due to those illnesses, nor did she learn to read or write. Nellie's family moved several times in her youth, always seeking work to support their family.

Nellie was 7 years old when she lost her mother, Nannie Chandler Williams, to influenza. Before her passing, Nannie (mom) tasked Nellie to protect her sisters and keep the family together. Nannie instilled Nellie with her faith, reminding her that God never gave you anything that you couldn't overcome.

At the same time, her father, Fred J. Morse, was diagnosed with tuberculosis and moved to a TB sanitarium for treatment. This left Nellie and her siblings to be placed with relatives and eventually an orphanage. Though confined to a chair, Nellie never lost faith and did her best to keep her siblings safe and at her side.

Nellie and her sisters were later reunited with her father, but times were hard in the beginnings of the Great Depression. Nellie didn't let these things stand in her way, always looking out for her siblings and family.

At the age of eight, Nellie's life was changed forever. An Indian medicine man approached her father and asked if he could help heal

Nellie of her polio. Nellie knew she had to walk again if she was to fulfill the promise she made to her mother before she passed.

Nellie believed sincerely in helping others, as so many had helped her over the years of her disability. Though only eight, she had lived a lifetime. True to his word, the Shaman faith-healed Nellie, instilling in her a personal commitment to a lifetime of service.

Having overcome her illnesses, Nellie began the long road to recovery with her unwavering faith. Though her life was filled with strife and contention, she always found time to be of service to others. Her inner strength and faith in God would support her for the rest of her life.

She knew firsthand the power of an education and impressed this upon her children, making sure that all of them graduated from school. Nellie was not afraid to speak her mind, with the strength of will to follow through on her convictions.

When confronted with an abusive spouse, Nellie was not afraid to leave with her children, even if that meant hitch hiking across the west to start anew in California. Nellie knew firsthand the destructive effects of poverty mixed with alcohol and drugs, witnessing this among the members of her tribe. She also instinctively knew that path lead to the grey fields of despair and desperation, and ultimately the loss of all hope.

Nellie refused to succumb to that siren call even though it was all around her, and she swore never to give in or give up. Nellie knew that Christ was there with her always; her strength when she faltered, there to lean on, and that Christ would carry her in those times she could not take another step.

From her father she learned carpentry and self-sufficiency, and built several homes including the one in California that she lived in until her passing. From her mother and grandmother, she learned the healing techniques of her tribe, of spirit walking and dream reading.

Nellie had many prophetic dreams, and she knew them for what they were. Though not always welcomed, she was gifted with this second sight. With Christ in her heart always, Nellie continued her path of service to others.

Nellie was a well-known Medicine woman at this time in California, and practiced her craft within the local community. Nellie loved to spend time in the mountains above her home, walking and hiking the sacred ground found there. It reminded her of the time spent with her father in the forests and mountains of her childhood.

When WWII broke out in the Pacific, Nellie was a constant fixture at the local Veterans center. Service to her country was part of her heritage, as members of her family fought alongside American soldiers in both the Indian wars of the early 1800's and in the Civil war that followed. As a child, Nellie was told stories of the sacrifice her family made in these wars for the benefit of future generations.

While still raising her growing family, Nellie helped in fundraisers, food and clothing drives, and in any other capacity needed. She won many awards for her selfless work from the Veteran's center. Nothing was too small for her to do when it came to supporting the returning vets.

When Nellie was in her sixties, she was diagnosed with congestive heart failure and given only a few months to live. Nellie now had grandchildren in school and it was important to her that they complete their education. She couldn't die now, and she prayed for help.

That night she had a dream. In it, she was walking on sacred land in the mountains above her home with Christ as her guide. Christ guided her to a field of white powder with Fern bush (Chamae Rose) medicinal plants glowing with vitality. Christ told her to make a tea with this plant and drink it several times a day.

When Nellie awoke, she knew just what to do. The location was well known to her, as were the medicinal herbs she was shown. And Nellie knew exactly where that field of white was.

Nellie immediately took a trip up into the mountains, against the advice of her family and friends to fulfill the quest that Christ had set upon her. Nellie returned invigorated with success, and with care and thanks, made the tea that Christ had shown her.

Within days, she felt better, and kept getting better each day. What was once thought to be the final weeks of her life turned into a miracle in the making.

A month later, she returned to her doctor for a checkup. Nellie's condition had improved so much that the doctor thought that they must have misdiagnosed her. In three months, Nellie was as healthy as ever, with no discernable heart condition.

This is just the tiniest glimpse of the life that Lady Nellie lived. But with this glimpse, one is better able to understand why the Andara crystals choose her as their first representative. The Andara crystals are about service to humanity, and found a kindred heart in Lady Nellie.

It was in 1967 that Lady Nellie found the first Andara crystal. She and her children were playing in the snow when one of her children hit her with a snowball, inside of which she found her first seafoam crystal. It was the only one found at the time and Nellie kept it in her home as a token from the earth and as a powerful healing crystal. Clearly she sensed its energy and began using it in her healings.

It was more than a decade later that a psychic healer came to Nellie for her knowledge as a medicine woman. Ally Keith came in search of new healing modalities; what she found was something much greater.

Ally had been having dreams of a green crystal of unheard of power. In her dreams, these crystals were of many colors, but it was the green ones that she was most attracted to. When Ally saw the green crystal on Nellie's altar, she became very excited.

"That's it! That's it!" Ally exclaimed and pointed to the green crystal. Ally told Nellie of her dreams and visions and asked her if she had any more in her possession. As a dream shaman, Nellie knew the power and truth that these visions can reveal.

At this time, no one had named this crystal yet, and Nellie explained how and when she found it and that it was the only one that had come off the mountain.

Ally knew there were more up there and explained to Nellie the importance of her find. "You just have to go back and get more, I'll buy everything you bring back, just please go back," Ally implored.

So Nellie and her grandchildren took a trip back into the mountains to look for more. Nellie proceeded to the area where the first one was found, but she and the grandchildren did not find any. It was a long drive to and from the mountain, and all their effort was for naught.

When Nellie arrived home, she contacted Ally and told her that they had not found any. Ally immediately told Nellie how important it was that she find them and was quite upset when Nellie balked at a return trip.

Nellie told Ally that they had searched high and low, and insisted that there were no other crystals up there. Nellie said "I've walked that property for 20 years and I know it like the back of my hand and 'there ain't no more crystals.' "

After they both calmed down, Ally convinced Nellie to try once more. What convinced Nellie was when Ally told her where and what to look for. Ally told her to look for a white power on the ground. Ally explained that it was "the dust of unicorns rubbing their horns together in play".

Nellie now knew where to look, as she was very familiar with that particular area from her previous visions. It was what she considered the most sacred part of the mountain, the area that Christ had shown her more than a decade ago.

So Nellie and the grandchildren returned to the mountain with a renewed purpose. She sought out the white powder as before, but could not see any crystals. Not to be deterred, she and the kids began digging in the powder and found clumps of something.

Being a medicine woman, Nellie knew that crystals could be covered in earth and unrecognizable. So she took one of these clumps and began to clean it off. As she wiped the dirt away, a beautiful crystal of light was revealed.

This area of the Sierra Nevada Mountains was well known for their obsidian deposits, and these had that same glass like structure. The difference was their brightness and variety of colors. Nellie had never seen obsidian like this, nor had she held crystals of such power.

Nellie thanked the mountain for sharing this gift, and she and the children collected all they could find. When they came down off the mountain, Nellie had collected hundreds of pounds of these obsidian-like crystals.

Nellie called Ally as soon as she reached home, excited to share this discovery with her. Ally was thrilled with the news, as Nellie told how and where they were discovered, like buried treasure.

Nellie told Ally that they had taken all that they could find and thought that was it. To which Ally replied, "The people of this planet are ready for the gifts of these crystals, so the earth will supply more very soon."

In less than a month, this prediction came true. An earthquake struck the area where these crystals were found and new parts of the mountain was uncovered. Nellie discovered this while checking if the earthquake had affected the property.

Nellie contacted Ally to pass on the news of this wonderful event. Ally said, "Gather what you can, someday the earth will take the crystals back to hold its seed."
A few years later, the prophetic sentence that Ally had spoken came to pass. Another

earthquake buried the site under tons of rock and dirt in the late 1980's.

Nellie and the children continued to gather what they could for the next ten years, but by the late 1990's, the surface sources were completely exhausted. Nellie persisted in her search for more, but what crystals could be found were small and few in number. Sometime in 1995, Nellie invited a channeler to do a reading on these new crystals.

There was at the time a small group of healers and light workers exploring these new and powerful crystals. A small gathering came together to listen and the name Andara was given to them by the channeled entity Thoth. From that day forward, these enigmatic tools were known as Andara crystals.

Then, in the spring of 2001, two teenage boys discovered a new cluster of crystals. These boys lived on an adjacent property to Nellie, and while gathering firewood on her land, came across them. They knew that Nellie collected these, as the families were close, and immediately presented their find to her.

Nellie was 86 by now, and her health was not as it had been just a few years ago. Visits and treks to her sacred mountain were almost physically impossible now. Her bout with polio as a child was manifesting in her legs again and made walking difficult.

Nellie made an offer to the boys to gather all of the crystals they could find and drive them to her home and she would pay them. The boys agreed, and a new chapter in the Andara crystal legacy began.

On June 25, 2010 Lady Nellie crossed over peacefully and has begun her next journey. Nellie's family and Mickey Magic will continue to protect her legacy and continue her mission of distributing the Andaras around the world.

The Science of Monatomic Andara Crystal

The goal of all scientific and metaphysical endeavors is to shed light on the unknown. What was once thought to be "metaphysical magic" is now commonplace. We live in a world that is rapidly changing, new discoveries seem to happen on a daily basis and what was believed to be immutable scientific fact has been turned on its head. So too has the discovery of Andara crystal expanded our knowledge of science and metaphysics.

A Sacred Discovery
In 1995, a unique mineral deposit was discovered near one of earth's high-energy vortex sites in the High Sierra Mountains of northern California. Monatomic Elements of Gold, Silver, Iridium, Rhodium, Chromium, Platinum, and other monatomic minerals were found in this deposit. This natural mineral complex exhibits extraordinary properties that strengthen and stabilize the electromagnetic fields of the human body.

Discovered within the deposit were glass-like crystals of exceptional power and beauty. Monatomic Andara crystal is a glass-like transmuted mineral complex from this naturally occurring mineral deposit high in monatomic minerals. The modalities of these crystals interact with the individual electromagnetically, restoring health and equilibrium.

Classical science teaches us that the three phases of matter are gasses, liquids, and solids. Current discoveries have now replaced that theory with the newer plasmas, condensates and liquid crystal states of matter. What classical science does not teach us (because these are new discoveries) is that there is, in fact, another phase of matter called "monatomic."

Monatomic (or monatomic) elements are the cutting edge of this new elemental frontier, yet its technology is ancient. The exotic properties of monatomic gold and the platinum group metals are rediscoveries of an advanced science understood and known by the ancient Mesopotamian, Egyptian and Israelite priests.

The ancient Mesopotamians called it shem-an-na and the Egyptians described it as mfkzt (moof-kooz-tee), vowels are omitted in the hieroglyph translation. Israelite priests called it manna, while the Alexandrians venerated it as a gift from Paradise and later chemists such as Nicolas Flamel called it the Philosophers' Stone.

The Monatomic Andara crystal is very special. In confirmed scientific testing of the location where they were originally found, the soil that Andara crystals were discovered in contain high levels of monatomic metallic elements.

Monatomic metallic elements are single atom metal elements that behave very differently than normal metals. First, as an example, monatomic gold is a fine white powder with very little weight, where metallic gold is very heavy. The atomic electron spin rate "frequency' in monatomic gold is much higher than gold. Very specialized equipment is needed to even test monatomic gold, as normal testing procedures produce inconclusive results or unknown substance.

When monatomic metallic elements are heated to high temperatures, they transmute to a glass like material, Andara crystal.

Monatomic elements have the following confirmed properties:
· Very high atomic spin rate or vibrational energy
· Like light photons, they pop in and out of existence
· Their vibrational energy can be passed to other objects
· They are first-matter elements, "prima matra"
· They have been used throughout history to heal and raise / expand consciousness . . .

A new science has emerged to deal with the quantum like properties of high spin state (high frequency) elements. Superconductivity, gravity defying materials, teleportation, space-time manipulation, multi-dimensional universes and other truly astonishing discoveries have been made and are projected theoretically for the near future.

Tests done in the U.S. and Russia confirm that monatomic metallic elements are superconductors with a null magnetic field, repelling both north and south magnetic poles. This is conducive to Zero-Point energy. 'Zero-Point Energy' (ZPE) is known as an energy that fills the fabric of all space, which exists at very high frequencies. Monatomic metallic elements have the ability to tap into this limitless supply of energy in ways we are just beginning to understand.

Most modern testing equipment is not sensitive enough to detect elements that are super-conductive in nature. When tested, most return inconclusive results and readings. Under spectroscopic analysis, monatomic metallic elements don't even register. Monatomic metallic elements have always exhibited the strange property of not being capable of analysis – they have been classified as substances unknown by testing labs.

It has also been shown that monatomic metallic elements can actually alter their physical state and shift into other dimensions. When heated under certain conditions, monatomic metallic elements, normally 35% silica, fuses into a beautiful obsidian-like material comprised of 75% silica (crystalline). Scientists are unable to explain how this seemingly impossible transmutation takes place. Other tests revealed that the material could transfer its exotic properties to similar metallic or silica materials. It seems that the monatomic metallic elements have the ability to resonate similar materials to their high frequency rate, transmuting and/or transforming that material to resemble and reflect their exotic properties.

Andara crystal is the result of monatomic metallic elements that are found naturally in the Etherium powders heated to high temperatures. This process not only transmutes the etherium powders, but refines the monatomic metallic metals and enhances their exotic properties. Testing has shown that Andara crystal resonates at the high frequency of the exotic matter they were created from.

Frequency is a measurement of energy. All substances can be measured for their wave signature or frequency. Even our thoughts are an energy that can be measured. Each organ of the body has its own frequency, with a particular range suggesting good health.

Bruce Tainio, of Tainio Technology (an independent division of Eastern State University) in Cheny, Washington, created a monitor to calculate bio-frequency. He found the average frequency of a healthy human body is between 62-68 Hz. Dr. Robert O'Becker (author of "The Body Electric") states "much about a person's health can be determined by the frequency of the person's body". If the frequency drops, the immune system is compromised. As that average of frequencies drops we start to see disease such as colds, flu, Epstein Barre virus, cancer, etc. On the other hand, higher frequencies denote physical health as well as highly creative and intuitive states.

In a test performed by Bruce Tainio, a subject was measured for frequency. Then the subject held a cup of coffee. The frequency dropped in seconds. After drinking the coffee, the frequency of the subject dropped again. The same tests were performed again, this time using positive and negative thoughts.

Within 3 seconds of thinking negative thoughts, the frequency dropped. It took 21 seconds of thinking positive thoughts to bring the frequency back up.

Bruce Tainio reported in 1997 that the Andara Crystal has been put on an electromagnetic spectrum analysis, and the electromagnetic patterns it emanates are not at all like regular obsidian. Bruce also tested the Etherium powder using the bio-frequency monitor and found unusual properties in the trace minerals. Andara Crystal is also heliocentric, meaning that it absorbs and reflects physical light toward the center of its crystalline spiral. Without elaborating on the science of heliocentric refraction, we will say here that this causes the Andara Crystal to be very healing to gaze into while holding in natural sunlight.

The Metaphysics of Monatomic Andara Crystals

The Andara Crystal was originally found by a half-Choctaw Indian woman by the name of Nellie, a Medicine Woman and Shaman. Being a Shaman and healer she immediately knew it had powerful healing properties. Her intuition was quickly borne out when various healings and other paranormal events started taking place.

Nellie immediately sent Rev. Maia a batch of the Andara Crystal, and she too had some rather profound spiritual experiences with it. This is the source translation of akashic record reading of Tehuti/Thoth by Rev. Maia Shamayyim-Nartoomid.

Tehuti "Andara is the name we have chosen to give to these crystals. They are composed primarily of "Prima Matra" (sacred matter) heated to very high temperatures. We have related to you in past transmissions that the "sacred matter" powders (referring to the "Etherium-Gold" and Prima Matra powder being sold as spiritual/nutritional supplements) coming from this sacred land were created by an inter-dimensional energy implosion. Those we call the "Timewalker", who worked in conjunction with the High Devas myth logically depicted as Unicorns, originally seeded the land for the formation of this Prima Matra. When the implosion occurred the 'seed' material was heated not only to very high levels but also in a contained "hyper-field" which is created by two dimensions touching. A hyper-field forms a "no-time" zone where linear laws of thermodynamics are warped or in some cases do not apply at all. It was within such a hyper-field that the Prima Matra powders and the Andara Crystals were originally created."

Tehuti "Approximately 2,000 years after the inter-dimensional implosion had occurred, a Lemurian temple complex was raised on this site. The name of this temple was 'Andara' meaning "Light of Beauty and Perfection". The primary purpose of this complex was in working with the Prima Matra powders, crystals and water of the land. By this we mean that through their purposeful interaction with the Prima Matra they effectively transmuted their crystalline DNA, therefore becoming a highly futurized from of "hue-man" being, even more developed in the Light matrix than the Lemurians of that age. Thus, we will cease calling these colonists

"Lemurians" and refer to them as "Andareans"."

Tehuti "Now we focus on the subject of the Andara Crystals. While they resemble a crystalline lava-glass and while certain similarities are present between lava-glass—such as obsidian and these crystals, they are vastly different energetically. Natural lava-glass could only be seen energetically as a distant cousin of Andara Crystals. Lava-glass is created from volcanic activity deep in the Earth, with the material coming to the surface in an eruption and being exposed to specific conditions as it cools. Because these lava-glass minerals come from deep inside the Earth within chambers containing great heat, they do contain various levels of Prima Matra.

Andara Crystals are even rarer than the Prima Matra lava-glass, in that they were formed inside a no-time hyper-field, creating within them a kinsothemitic continuum. This continuum that allows a moving time field within the elemental and structural composition of the crystal formation. In essence, this 'K' continuum does not align to natural polarity. Instead, it phase-matches directly with the Universal Light matrix, or the 'Golden Net' of Athena. (Note: Athena's Net is the geometric space-time continuum, a.k.a. 'The Web of Athena'.)"

Being heliocentric, the Andara crystal tends to draw the individual's consciousness into the center of the energy spiral within when they gaze into the crystal, thus bringing that person's consciousness into more intimate contact with the Andarean consciousness. Andara crystal also creates a double vortex, in other words they have zero point energy and they have super-conductive monatomic energy.

It has been our experience that the field associated with the Andara Crystal represents an unlimited kinetic potential. It works quite differently than regular crystals like quartz, where one may amplify their intention through the crystal. Instead, one inserts their intention into the kinetic field associated with the Andara Crystal and the ENTIRE field moves in response to that intention.

Since Andara crystals were first discovered, many people working with them have experienced major shifts in their lives. Richard B., a medical intuitive, in Vancouver, WA, writes, "...the individual using the Andara crystal is able to raise their own vibration to match, receive, and mediate the higher frequencies. Meditating with Monatomic Andaras, using gem elixirs made from them, carrying them, and working with them in other ways will help us to attune to them and increase our ability to use them as tools for healing and the science of exploring our consciousness..."

Many stewards that have adopted Andara crystals always comment on the energy field that is almost tangible, a whoosh that seems to go through them bringing relief and joy. They feel lighter, relaxed and surrounded by light. Physical pain is reduced, or dissolved. Vitality and optimism seem abundant. Others report an expansion of consciousness, of oneness with God.

The Monatomic Andara Experience

Andara crystals positively affect the energy patterns that move through the body's meridians. Andara crystals initiate electromagnetic balance and harmony via a positive-charged wave that restores and cleanses. The individual is blessed with greater creativity, enhanced mind body coordination, improved learning ability and less stress. Calmness and serenity can also result as mental clutter gives way to a more focused thought process.

The energy of Andara crystals is specific to the upper chakra centers. Thoughts become more focused, and the transformational process of energy (intent) into matter is accentuated. The vibrational difference between thought, and the object of the thought, becomes reduced. Therefore, the time and conscious effort required to manifest intent into physical reality is also reduced.

Many experience the effects of Andara crystals as dramatically expanded sensory perception and access to information beyond normal third dimensional channels. Intuition is increased, especially experiences of telepathic connection with other people or beings. Connections to your higher divine self are strengthened, increasing feelings of universal oneness, harmony and joy.

Andara crystals are a soul enhancing, high vibrational healing tool that works on all levels; physical, emotional, and spiritual. The process creates a unique healing experience, individual for each person, assisting him or her in releasing unwanted energies while expanding their understanding of their true reality, closer to their original divine consciousness.

Andara is a master crystal, a healer and a powerful tool for: (1) increasing awareness and vibration to access universal knowledge; (2) cleaning and balancing chakras; (3) activates one's energy-channeling ability; (4) accelerates the spiritual development process, and (5) aids a person to manifest the life s/he chooses.

Andara Crystals have been placed at all the sacred sites on the planet, in the temple and the pyramid in Egypt. They have created a healing field surrounding this planet. Each Andara Crystal connects and links with all the others, and the sites and information at that location is available to those who can connect with their hearts and minds.

To date: true Andara crystals have been found in high-energy vortex sites in the Sierra Mountain region of northern California and reportedly in South Africa.

Andara Crystal Myths, Legends and Truths.

I have been interested in rocks, stones, crystals, etc since I was young. That could be explained away as what my Capricorn earth sign would imply, but that interest over time became a passion and now I know why. As everything is energy, crystals in particular hold higher frequency and if you can match their frequency you can effectively program / imbue / ask the crystal to amplify your intent. Being around crystals as much as I have over the years gave me ample opportunity to put them to the test and when I was in alignment with a crystal it definitely worked for me. I spent an enormous amount of time and resources to learn about each crystal, found the right books and internet sites detailing each particular stone, learned crystal impact on chakra alignment and acquired many pieces, most to pass along to others who needed them. I consider myself well-versed in crystals and the power they possess.

As my journey continued, my interest in crystals became more metaphysically entangled. So my extensive collection of various types of crystals became more focused on Moldavite (dimensional connections), Labradorite (magick), Quartz (super amplifier), Sugilite (violet ray- type unconditional love).

And then Andara Crystals crossed my path.

As much as I had a wide-spread awareness of crystals, I had no knowledge of Andaras. In July of 2018, my divinely inspired education was about to begin.

I have a dear friend we'll call Shannon, who among her skills is a gifted Reiki healer. Her sensitivities to energies (holding crystals and feeling their energy for example) was something I envied. So, I thought given our common appreciation for crystals I would find something special that would compliment her reiki environment. I don't recall why it was green that I searched for but near the top of the eBay results was an "Emerald Shift Andara". It was beautiful to see. As I read the description about what an Andara crystal was a capable of, I thought – this sounds like just the thing. I had no frame of reference about Andara costs (nor anything else about Andaras for that matter) so the $175.00 the seller was asking didn't seem unreasonable. So I bought my first Andara … or so I thought.

When it arrived it was a beautiful piece and the color was vivid. I saw Shannon within a few days and I was eager to see her reaction especially as it pertained to whatever energy she could report it exchanged with her. When the moment finally arrived, pretty as it may be, she didn't really sense anything. That certainly wasn't inconclusive as neither of us had any experience with them before and so maybe we weren't on the right same vibration. But something just felt off.

Upon further research on Andaras in general, there was plenty of scuttlebutt on the Internet regarding fake Andaras being sold. "Slag glass" was being passed off as Andaras. I didn't want to believe that I got taken so I let it simmer for a few days and at the end of that time my intuition was saying: Yes, you got taken. Regardless of these unpleasant circumstances, I had a drive, that became a quest, to find out about what Andaras are. So when I want to learn everything I can about a subject, you can be assured that at the end – comprehensive due diligence has been completed, ask anyone who knows me. Between the feeling of being taken advantage of and the drive to learn everything – the dog was let off the leash.

It would take almost two years for the circle of knowledge to fully illuminate my comprehension of Andara Crystals. (See the

results of my research here:
https://40kftview.com/andara-crystals/)

What my journey was directing me to remember is that this exercise wasn't so much about the crystals themselves as it was about rediscovering Etherium, the mineral rich deposit in which it is formed and what it can do.

I performed an exhaustive search of everything I could find on Andaras, their history, the people associated with them, their metaphysical properties, color variations, availability ... everything. It took a while for my research to gel and patch together what we have a record of. Remember, this substance wasn't even on the radar until 1967, obviously it has been here MUCH longer than that. Among the names synonymous with Andaras are Lady Nellie and Mickey Magic. There are others who have had relationships with Nellie during her life, but I have had the opportunity to spend quality time with Mickey and his son Alex to hear about 25 years around Nellie, the property, Andara crystals and Etherium.

Much of what I'm sharing came from Mickey's extraordinary life around these relics. His book will be coming out soon and Andaras are only one fascinating dimension of this dear brother of mine.

Let's correct some misconceptions so that we can fully appreciate what Andaras and etherium are.

- Andaras were found in the Mount Shasta area. As much as I love Mt Shasta and I would love this to be true, it is not accurate. I can share with you that it is in that area of the Sierra Mountains. More than that, I am understandably not allowed to share.
- The property is located is in high desert area, meaning summers are triple digit hot and winters are cold with snow. Mickey shared that the way Nellie found her first seafoam Andara was when she was hit with it inside a snowball one of her kids chucked at her.

Authenticity

If you know the story of how moldavite came to form on Earth https://www.crystalvaults.com/crystal-encyclopedia/moldavite, then it's reasonable to understand how matter with a unique energetic signature can find its way to our planet. This of course happened during a meteor strike with such mass and force that the resulting melted earth/space dust spewed back out from the core and scattered near the Moldau River in Czechoslovakia where it cooled into the forms you see today.

I mention Moldavite because of the similarities they share with Andara material in that both were created under great heat-stress fusing material not originating from the planet. As such, there is a finite amount of said material. That however, is where the similarities between Andaras and Moldavite (or any other crystal for that matter) end. The energetic signatures that these two crystals have are HIGH frequency and they are meant to be portals to dimensional access given the correct alignment. But the monatomic material in Andara matter is prima matra ... like nothing else on Earth.

So as for authenticity (and pleading ignorance to the existence of Andara matter in South Africa,) there is only one place that Andara crystals and Etherium can come from and it's this deposit in the Sierra Mountains. Without etherium, Andaras don't exist as that is the matter they are created from. Again, I cannot speak to the existence of Andaras in South Africa, but the Northern California deposit – that is only other possible source of this crystal and substance.

If you have the least amount of sensitivity toward energy you will immediately connect to the strong presence of an Andara. It really shouldn't be called a crystal because it carries consciousness of connectedness to higher dimensions. When you connect to an Andara you are not asking it to imbue and amplify your intent upon it as you would a crystal, you actually exchange energy – yours and its. Now can you appreciate what kind of universal network of Akashic information you are connected with? And by now the Andaras have been gridded around the Earth.

Sadly, if you have been sold on the idea that an Andara came from anywhere else than that I've described, you've been mislead. That doesn't begin to address all the pretty glass that people who know better have been selling as Lady Nellie property crystals. I can see how it happened over time as there is only a finite amount of Andaras in the world at this time, without breaking larger pieces into smaller. So when you can't get more to sell ... how do you backfill to meet demand? By selling something that looks similar. But there is no mistaking the energy of an authentic Andara vs anything else. That is the true test. My advice for those who seek to adopt and steward an Andara (they are not museum pieces, they are healing tools), is to visit a source and let them speak to you because they will. Andaras however, have a stunning visual presence that can jump off the screen at you when you connect to a picture of them.

Price
The going wholesale price of Andaras today is:
($600/lb) $37.50 oz

($800/lb) $50.00 oz – Elders

Expect to pay somewhere between $2-3 retail per gram, depending on the quality and uniqueness of the crystal.

So let's use the two I bought online as examples (told ya the dog was off the leash): I've made a habit of copy and pasting the information about crystals mainly to learn myself what features the crystal possesses, but its a habit I've developed for things I have bought on eBay.

(1) What follows is the description of the Emerald Shift Andara as it was listed on eBay:

[This color of Lady Nellie Monatomic Andara crystal has chosen the name Emerald Shift. Emerald is the color of the deep, verdant forest, untouched and abound with hidden secrets. Emerald Shift unveils our inner world of sacred wisdom and insights, ushering in the "Age of Transparency". This crystal has been a part of my personal collection and healing practice for years, and I am sad to see her go, but she tells me that it is time for her to move on to help others. She has brought much abundance, joy, understanding and healing to all of the lives that she has touched.

She has always been charged under the full moon and cleansed ritually with sage to keep her vibrations at the highest level.

This crystal weights 290g. She is a showstopper and a marvelous display piece of museum quality. The heliocentric swirls in this crystal pull you deep down into her crystal clear depths, glittering like a diamond and filling you with love and cosmic wisdom. The clarity of this piece is just stunning. Words fail to do her any justice. She is breathtaking. The swirls and rainbows in her just make her even more heavenly with shimmering iridescence. Andaras are used to access to higher dimensions of consciousness. Andaras will open and cleanse each chakra and will detoxify any form of negativity. The healing vibrations are amazing and truly from another world. The Andaras will help increase your access to all Universal knowledge and will greatly accelerate your spiritual development. Andara is one of the best crystals for giving one the ability to channel. Andaras are also powerful healers and activators. Andara crystals are ancient healing crystals that have been around for many moons and are believed to have been used in the healing temples of Atlantis & Lemuria, but only now in recent years are they being recognized in the western world as a powerful healer and ascension tool for spiritual advancement.

They are all Heliocentric which simply means they absorb and reflect light which is why they have become such a popular choice for healers and collectors. (Human reasoning was close with that conclusion: however, Andaras have consciousness – they absorb and exchange Light energy.) In 1995, a unique mineral deposit was discovered near one of earth's high-energy vortex sites in the High Sierra Mountains of northern California. Monatomic Elements of Gold, Silver, Iridium, Rhodium, Chromium, Platinum, and other monatomic minerals were found in this deposit. This natural mineral complex exhibits extraordinary properties that strengthen and stabilize the electromagnetic fields of the human body. Discovered within the deposit were glass-like crystals of exceptional power and beauty. Andara crystal is a glass-like transmuted mineral complex from this naturally occurring mineral deposit high in monatomic minerals.

The modalities of these crystals interact with the individual electromagnetically, restoring physical and metaphysical health through energetic equilibrium.

The Andara crystal is very special. In confirmed scientific testing of the location where they were originally found, the soil that Andara crystals were discovered in contain high levels of monatomic metallic elements. Monatomic metallic elements are single atom metal elements that behave very differently than normal metals. First, as an example, monatomic gold is a fine white powder with very little weight, where metallic gold is very heavy. The atomic electron spin rate "frequency' in monatomic gold is much higher than gold. Very specialized equipment is needed to even test monatomic gold, as normal testing procedures produce inconclusive results or unknown substance.

When monatomic metallic elements are heated to high temperatures, they transmute during fusion into a glass-like material, Andara crystal. Monatomic elements have the following confirmed properties:

· Very high atomic spin rate or vibrational energy
· Like light photons, they pop in and out of existence
· Their vibrational energy can be passed to other objects
· They are first-matter elements, "prima matra"
· They have been used throughout history to heal and raise / expand consciousness.

Being heliocentric, the Andara crystal tends to draw the individual's consciousness into the center of the energy spiral within when they gaze into the crystal, thus bringing that person's consciousness into more intimate contact with the Andarean consciousness. Andara crystal also creates a double vortex, in other words they have zero point energy and they have super-conductive monatomic energy.

It has been our experience that the field associated with the Andara Crystal represents a very large kinetic potential. It works quite differently than regular crystals like quartz, where one may amplify their intention through the crystal. Instead, one inserts their intention into the kinetic field associated with the Monatomic Andara Crystal and the ENTIRE field moves in response to that intention.]

Clearly, the seller had done their homework on the content relating to Andara crystal characteristics with a sentimental twist. Had I known more about the value of Andaras at the time ... the price should have been a red flag.

Let's compare shall we?
If this were an authentic 290g piece I should have expected to pay $2-3 per gram retail: thus making the value = $580-870. Knowing what I know the lower of the two value would have been in line with fair market ... why only $175.00?

(2) This piece is a blue Andara I purchased online through a site that had convinced me of their authenticity and although I am satisfied that the crystal is authentic – I have to wonder why such a piece weighing 18 oz would be priced as listed and then deeply discounted. This source's content would demonstrate the expertise that they know an Andara from a non-Andara.

This 18 oz piece @ wholesale should have been $675.00 as opposed to the $494.00 it was listed at for sale.

Sources
Now would be a good time to tell you about how synchronicities magically aligned and put me in places to see authentic Andaras from Nellie's parcel with people that have been around the crystals and Nellie for years.

By the time I arrived in Mt Shasta that Sunday last July it was mid-afternoon so the remainder of the day would be checking in and settling in at the place I was going to stay in Weed, CA. Then I thought I would drive to the town of Mt Shasta and get familiar with what was where. Main Street had a stretch of storefronts, restaurants and miscellaneous services – this would be a good place to start. You don't have to ask me twice if I'd like to visit a crystal shop and there were a few to explore. I started at the north end and worked my way south, stopping at each crystal shop, making note of Blue Star Child Gallery (I chose not to stay that day, but knew I would return to explore Haruko's gallery space soon).

The Crystal Room was the last place I visited as it was not directly on the main drag (and someone had to tell me it's whereabouts). High on my list of places to visit, my research had resulted in learning that authentic Andaras from Lady Nellie's property were within this shop. It was later in the afternoon when I finally arrived at the shop. There were people in pockets throughout the nine rooms that make up the footprint. Some admiring the crystals, some the artwork, some the crystal bowls, there was a brisk amount of activity of some interesting variety. I wandered by myself taking in all the positive energy in this place. The crystals were stunning and there is something for everyone here. But I was in search of something specific ... Andaras. The last corner of the last room I explored had a rather small display of mostly seafoam and root beer Andaras of various sizes. My mind hoped ... there certainly must be more. I could see that trying to attract the attention of someone from the shop with whom I could ask questions ... this was not the time.

Two days later, I returned around noon. I wandered around the shop scoping out maybe a section of Andaras I had missed while trying to catch the eye of Bev. By now I'd learned that Beverly is the owner and manager of the shop and has been an institution for years. When I finally got the chance to ask her about Andaras, she said "Oh, I have lots of Andaras, they are down in the Shire.

I'm the only one in the shop today, but I'm taking a customer and a few of his friends down there tonight at 6PM after I close the shop. If you'd like to come along, you are more than welcome". I was there at 5:55PM, if there was an opportunity for me to see a collection of authentic Andaras – just tell me where to be and when – I will be there. I can only imagine that there probably not a lot of people who had the opportunity to see what I got to see. Beverly had acquired a collection that filled rows of shelves filled with boxes of every kind of Andara, not to mention the larger elder pieces that sat on the floor. From the moment the door to Shire opened ... I felt a surge of energy like a breeze as I passed through. It turns out that her customer that day was Ted Mahr. At the time I didn't know Ted and he certainly didn't know me, but I owe him thanks because without his visit the opportunity to tag along probably wouldn't have come along. (Or would it have?)

Bev couldn't have been more patient with the small entourage with Ted, I was looking for a violet or indigo colored crystal (or so I thought). While I went through box after box, Bev handed me a just smaller than fist sized "root beer shaman" Andara, shaped like a wedge. It had a beautiful amber highlighted eye in the center with amber Easter eggs everywhere when the light hit from different angles. Almost as though it was a predetermined outcome, the crystal was going with me and I was definitely connected. The energy was grounding, clearly what I needed from this visit ... so Starbuck's wedge has kept me grounded (and so much more) on every adventure I've been on ever since.

You don't have to dig very deeply into Andaras before you come across the name Mickey Magic. What I learned about Mickey from his website, YouTube interviews and other sources confirm that Mickey (and his son Alex) have been as integral in Andaras finding their way around the globe as was Nellie. Mickey and only a very few others had visited the property itself, but he had helped her harvest and distribute what was discovered in the deposit on her land when Nellie realized exactly it was that she was given stewardship of. Her higher self had given her guidance that the time for Andaras to grid the planet was upon us ... and that is what she and Mickey set out to do.

Originally, Mickey and I had connected by way of mutual connections and when Telos became a topic of high common interest, I was invited to his compound in the Santa Cruz mountains where he had maintained a crystal spiral of Andara Elders with such an energetic state – this is either a play land of consciousness energy or a minefield for the uninitiated. So I had been finishing up restoring the Ascension Handbook on the website and needed a break after two solid days of coding. Mickey popped up as some FB reminder on my phone and I thought to myself ... "let's see about visiting Mickey this weekend". Within a few hours on Thursday, I was heading for Santa Cruz to spend the weekend potentially in a tent next to the Andara Spiral. I spent four days that went like a blur with Mickey, his family and members of the tribe who came around while I was there. There is magic here in the Enchanted Forest.

Here on this property is what remains of Mickey's collection of relics and archive of pieces yet to be adopted. There is no more to be extracted from the place where they were found at this time. Aside from some private collections ... Mickey and The Crystal Room remain the only two places where authentic Lady Nellie Andaras can be found and handled. There are other sources to buy them online and I will list those that I know have acquired them from Mickey or The Crystal Room in order to be certain that you are actually purchasing an Andara. By now, I am sure you can appreciate that they didn't cross your path by accident and they are not for everyone.

Anyway the trip was magical and the compound felt like home. Mickey and I didn't meet as much as we gladly reconnected from some other time. I spent another four days around the Memorial Day with Mickey and a smaller circle of tribe members and continued exploring the Akash regarding Etherium. That is a topic that deserves separate focus, but critical for you to understand what is an Andara.

Here is a list of sites that I can confirm you can find authentic Andaras:
https://www.mickeymagic.com
You can contact Mickey through the website. You can also make arrangements to visit the compound near Santa Cruz, CA

The Crystal Room is available at their brick and mortar location in Mt Shasta, CA.

2021 Jun - Dimensional experience - Return to the Telos portal hike, meet at the entrance with She-Ah-Ma

After adjusting schedules I'd be back in Shasta the 3rd Thursday for at least a few weeks and during that time, explore the area with tribe to share sacred energetic portals, re-connect with others in the area to compare notes on individual ascension signs and find "me" time on the mountain now that everything should be open and accessible. As I always do when I first arrive in Mt Shasta, I make the drive as far on Everett Memorial Highway as conditions allow. There was no more snow, in fact, I've not seen the mountain from this perspective with zero snow and that's precisely what I was seeing. In spite of clear conditions, the re-opening of the road that seasonally gets gated from Bunny Flat to access the Old Ski Bowl trailhead summit parking lot among other places along the 3.3 mile stretch didn't happen. Ok then, I know what I have to do to reach my destination – hike it from Bunny Flat and I'd return to begin by 9AM Friday morning.

In preparation for this hike, I had to factor in things I knew and variables I did not – I knew that the road was going to be closed, meaning if that's the route I choose, its a 3.3(+) mile walk with a change in altitude from 6919' to 8120'. I was convinced that a route more "as the crow flies" would be shorter and much more pleasant through the forest than just following the road. I had the Lat:Long coordinates from someone who read my accounts, figured out where the portal was and then found it by making that hike from Bunny Flat back in May from where he took pictures and screen capped the compass coordinates. I've kept a lid on that information since and shared it with only a few before I had a chance to return.

Using the Lat:Long on Google Maps / Google Earth was helpful – if I was driving. In spite of changing the mode of travel to hiking it just kept wanting to reroute me to the road (aarrgghhhh), so I just bagged the whole Google Map option. I remembered using a Cal Topo map online last year the very first day of my hiking and to say it was helpful is an understatement considering I was wandering in places I'd never been "off-trail". For some incomprehensible reason the mobile signal in a lot of (not every) places around Mt. Shasta is decent. Between downloading this tool and my phone's compass, I could see where I was and what direction I should head.

Drawing a visual line between where I stood at Bunny Flat and Mt Shasta in the distance was my line. So off I headed on some paths that headed that way. Soon to stay on-line, I ventured off-trail but came to a marked trail labeled "Snow Bunny Trail" that I decided to follow for a bit. Just north of that (see coordinates) I found the first of 5 portals I was supposed to visit / discover. Remember, I asked my guides to "show me the way" and this is the direction I took. Among those variables I didn't take into account were the elevation changes in unknown forest. So I just kept looking up the mountain knowing I had to ascend and followed intuition.

As you can see on the Google map I plotted all of the vortexes that I had screen capped – I went WAY north and later it would result in me having to descend only to have to ascend again ☐. I showed you all the vortexes I exchanged energy at to share my experience. These places are all "off-trail" with the exception of the first one just past Snow Bunny Trail and that one is relatively easy to find and well worth the hike. (The Telos portal is the right-most dropped pin)

So I continued to hike as the crow flies to Shastina from Bunny Flats to find the energetic portal to Telos I had experienced that Sunday last July.

Left Bunny Flats @ 9ish
Reached the perch @ 1ish

First: I returned to the scene a different being than I was last year. I have some new "upgrades" since the last visit and it's clear as anything to me now as to why. My ability to sense and "see" energies has been greatly enhanced / elevated. Those energy vortexes radiate and in my case it's as though I can "see" the etheric aura around the object.

I'll pause here for a moment to give you some clarity and try to explain the "upgrades". Along my journey, tools / people / resources have been placed in my path for my use. The next to the last weekend in February, 2018, I participated in an Ayahuasca journey where Mother Ayahuasca said I was the Protector of Gaia. She showed me visions of new Earth where I had my 5th dimensional abilities restored to me. I was a Master Alchemist and Sorcerer / Wizard with a crystal that had the power to heal heart space immediately and transmute negative energy into Light. The crystal manifested as an Andara Crystal (Epiphany) and if you know me, you know what I've learned about Andaras and Etherium. Some of the difficult to decipher information in Thoth's Emerald Tablets that he left behind are coming into focus for those that are ready. But enough about that for now. On to the Telos portal.

When I finally reached the normally highly active area, one thing was "smack you in the face" different this time – there was no one else here. My frame of reference for this three-level parking area attached to several popular trailheads was active every time I had been here no matter what day or time. Right now – I had the entire place to myself. I didn't see another soul until the descent on the road near the Panther Meadows campsite.

This visit – the energy signature at the portal site was noticeably much higher frequency and this time I could see the energetic outline of where the last opening took place. I was about to sit on the ground in this space and exchange energy I brought along – I had looked forward to that the entire hike. Then that multidimensional breeze ... it must be an energetic release ... and the portal was again open. I got to see She-Ah-Ma today at the portal. She came as far as the opening but not out.

So I sat with my legs spread saddle-like on the square bolder directly in front of the opening and had an extraordinary opportunity to chat with her. I was buzzing from the inter dimensional energy around us all and there were a number of influences inside me as well causing what I was feeling in that moment.

When I first heard her voice I recognized it right away, it is melodious. "So they call you Starbuck", she said in the most endearing way possible. I just wanted to keep listening to her voice. She makes a striking vision. She's wearing this blingy green ensemble that reflected the light like a hologram – so cool. Never mind she is 8+ ft tall so I look up at her a lot ☐.

She started by asking what I thought now that the Prima Matra has found its way back into the hands of a Master Alchemist. What we discussed will stay secret for now.

I wanted to know why we were meeting here with her feet almost back on Terra Firma. I wondered for a moment why she wouldn't step out and then it occurred to me that she can't pass into this realm without dropping her vibration to match this environment and why would anyone want to do that as reascending is not a simple thing? She reminded me – I did.

I wanted more insight on specifically my time in Telos and she said it is already beginning to come back to you. I asked if I have a name I go by in Telos and she said that would also come to me, but in the meantime she's fond of Starbuck.

We spent a significant amount of time then it seemed just looking at the mountain saying nothing but knowing this is Endgame for 3D and with the time remaining we are going to enjoy it as is while we can.

Said our farewells knowing I had to walk over 3 miles (following the road this time) to return to the Bunny Flat parking lot. I began climbing back down and as I dropped down a level, the portal is still open. I reached for my phone to capture a pic and too late – it was off again! At least this time I could fire my iPhone up right away. Wouldn't you know it, as soon as my phone was powered back up – yeah no more portal that's I could see through my lens.

It's no coincidence that all of this was happening whether I paid attention to the fact that this timed itself to occur at Summer Solstice or not. Once it was within my awareness, it was just one more synchronous 2 by 4 upside my metaphysical head to bring attention to what was aligning. Plenty of other extraordinary things were unfolding for me and everyone else it seemed in my orbit on an accelerated timeline. Awareness of this tribe's orbit was growing exponentially as was the tribe itself as a result of many factors influencing it.

Through the first part of July, as those changes were manifesting into each one of us … that same question kept getting asked: "ok, so now what do we do with what we know / can do".

2021 Jul - Dimensional experience - Airbnb Farmhouse Robbinsdale AL Elias the Artist visit

When I returned to Santa Rosa from Mt Shasta, I had plenty to assimilate. Things surfaced that needed to be resolved or dissolved. Cords to cut. Vibration to hold. Alignment to maintain. One of those cords to either cut or snug up required a trip to Alabama where a piece of my heart still had space. It's a part of my personal space I don't share with others and I only make this exception as it set the stage for a multidimensional encounter in a rural Alabama Airbnb farmhouse.

I thought I was going to potentially restart a relationship, that the two of us had been communicating about for a few weeks by now. We had met while I was consulting in Louisiana and the time we spent together was special. It was time to have this discussion face to face, so I made arrangements to take in consideration the driving distance, her schedule and a quiet place to meet as soon as possible. In the end, I learned I was going there for different purposes.

CA is a CNA in a busy rural hospital in western Alabama. She is a Capricorn, a Service to Others being and doesn't like being idle. She works three consecutive 12 hour 7P-7A shifts beginning Sunday. In spite of drastic shortages in staffing at her place of employment, supervision with less than the utmost regard for her contributions and little to say about conditions other than just comply to keep your job ... she loves her work and the people she helps. The plan was ... I'd arrive Tuesday night at the farmhouse and be there when she got off work around 7:30A the next morning. I'd be here until the next

Sunday so we had 5 days together to see what was in store for us.

When she arrived the next morning I helped her unload but I was fully aware she'd be exhausted after working 36 of the last 72 hours. It wasn't like I hadn't just driven 2300+ miles to get here – so we decided to just catch up on rest. When we started stirring late afternoon to get up and around, it made sense to just spend time on the couch, watch movies and reconnect. But she woke with a bit of a headache in the afternoon and she felt like she was getting a bit congested. She explained that the last night of the three, her floor became a Covid level overnight as the Delta variant just happened to make its appearance while I was there. In retrospect, she is fairly certain she knows which patient she assisted coughed in the wrong manner and to make a lengthy few days short – by Thursday we had confirmation from her work that she tested positive. By mid afternoon Friday she tried to tough it out as I had come a long way but her symptoms were getting more acute and it only made sense that she return home to her own bed with her comforts around her and begin to work through the recovery process. It should be noted that at no time during this period around her did I experience any ailments at all and to make certain, had a Covid test in Baton Rouge on Tuesday that came back negative. There are a variety of reasons why I know I wasn't susceptible to sickness and I never really gave it a second thought. In my understanding any virus needs to find a malady to compromise – my system doesn't have any.

Now I told you that story to tell you this story: Friday after CA left – I lost it. I cried out 'WTF Universe ...' ? What am I doing in a rural farmhouse in Alabama? Because it certainly wasn't what I thought I was coming here for. From 5-10PM I laid on the day bed with the TV providing white noise, where she had spent most of the week slipping in and out of sleep – hoping I could get some rest of my own. I must have finally dozed off and was facing the back of the day bed, when just before midnight my higher senses were coming online. During multidimensional experiences I have, the environment always seems to carry the scent of sage. It's always sage. And I was sensing it now.

I turned around to face the room and there he is, sitting in a chair at the table so I see him seated in profile. The Etherium is open and he's mixing red with white. He is wearing a simple hooded frock that looked hemp-like and looked what I expect Merlin would look like. Long white hair and flawless features.

Who are you?
[My name is Elias, I'm here to answer to your call. Know that you have multidimensional resources you can command when you are in alignment. I came to offer my support and pay my respects to a Sage: the Protector of Gaia. Summon your strength – we're almost there. You know what you carry inside of you from the Andara spiral. Use it.

- You're about to prove to yourself your powers of transmutation – it was one of the unconscious reasons for your trip. Heal your loved ones is who you are – remember? She could use your skill set mindful that she is in total control of her being. You are here to heal her.

Keep your vibration high, many who don't realize it yet will be counting on you to explain ascension and what they will go through very soon. But you know that and I'm here to share a potion Alex suggested with white and red Etherium. You will remember the formula once you've experienced it, but you don't need it. You already know the alignment of your heart core and Source. But so you will have something to remember this moment between us by, take this. Lie back, close your eyes and in a moment- you will feel a sensation from your core through your crown.]

Add Clairkinetic (the ability to feel the angels, guides and beings in other dimensions, getting a physical sensation in or on the body to indicate that another presence is making a connection) to the list of newly recalled abilities. ☐

During that journey I spent time in Merlin's chamber seeing Alchemy and Magick. Saturday, the next morning: a YouTube lecture on "Alchemy as a Key to Social

Regeneration by Manly P Hall" came to my awareness and connected the dots on who is Elias the Artist (Elias Artista)

Elias the Artist is mentioned at the 30:07 mark in the presentation and it goes as such: ["In the old Alchemical system there was a mysterious being called Elias the Artist. Elias is the patriarch referred in the Bible as one who went to God without death. And this mysterious power – Elias the Artist would come in the night to some alchemist who was considered worthy and would give him the secret or forgive him perhaps a few grains of the elixir of life or the transmutation. Would stay a little time and then disappear and never be seen again. And in each case the Elias power left some proof behind it. It left evidence to the chemist himself that there was an answer. That there was a solution. And in some cases as in the case of Sendivogius, this powder actually was used by him to transmute base metals and apparently physically he believed at least that it accomplished this end. Or was it true that Sendivogius also knew and put into symbolism what this powder really was. That it was not there to transmute base copper, bronze or iron but to transmute base ignorance, superstition or fear into the realization of truth."] Taking the time to listen to the actual presentation is well worth it to fully understand these types of connections between dimensional beings.

2021 Aug 6-7 - Dimensional experience - Santa Cruz, CA Mickey Magic's compound Light being activation Kumu

I was expected back in the Santa Cruz mountains by Friday and that gave me a few days of Divine time with family in Baton Rouge. When I arrived back at Mickey's compound sometime mid afternoon things were about to be put into motion I didn't see coming for me. I was about to make the acquaintance of an Old Hawaiian Kumu (teacher) who was intentionally placed in my path. I hadn't met her before and knew nothing about her, but she knew about me, my dimensional Telos experience and things about myself I didn't yet know. She planned to be at Mickey's that day where unbeknownst to me, we would finally meet. Now Mickey and Kumu had history and they have worked together in their healing work especially using Andaras. Her purpose is to use her gifts to "Malama the Aina" Malama = Heal; Aina = Land.

After a pleasant afternoon with everyone on the deck at Mickey's – where life in the Enchanted Forest takes place, around 5PM, Kumu invites me over to where she's near some huge healthy plants and taking pictures.

The pictures are capturing Light Beings she's called and she is able to photograph them among the leaves. She tells me to stand with my arms around the plant's auric energy and she continues to take pictures. Moments later, she shared the images she had just taken with me and sent them to me. They showed a physical Light interaction between myself and the being. Later I will learn, that this was a test of some type and without having satisfied this condition ... what was to follow wouldn't have transpired.

I could "hear" the vibration when these beings are in the vicinity and it took a few experiences for me to realize that. In terms of the Light itself as you will see ... it is quite visible to the naked eye and dense.

That was Friday. We had plans the next day to spend some time working on updating Mickey's site to make the acquisition of Andaras easier for everyone. Then there came a call mid-morning – Kumu is returning. No one at the time knew why but she would be here just after noon.

Now Kumu usually travels with an entourage of students and colleagues, but today it was just her and one student. When she arrived, they brought a feast of Chinese food suited to feed dozens and a number of protective travel cases. These cases held artifacts that few people ever get to see, much less hold or photograph. They were 30K+ years old and had codes inscribed everywhere on them that appeared Ancient. Three of these relics were ceremonial pipes that were about to be put to use. Kumu had brought some sacred medicine from her ancestral land in Hawaii that was going to help guide me – we were about to go through a ceremony establishing further contact with higher dimensional Light Beings on the Andara Spiral.

Late in the afternoon, Kumu invited Mickey and I down to the spiral to stand behind the angel statue next to the Goddess Stone in the center. While we were there she photographed the phenomenon around us documenting different apparitions of how dense the Light Beings were.

Immediately after we were sitting on the wall along the side of the spiral and she continued to capture what dimensional phenomenon was occurring. This time the light was different and a blue light swept into place. At first glance it looks as though I am holding something with both hands ... and what it captured was a serpent form representing Shiva rising to protect me.

As much as it all sounds like it should mean something at this point in time, I've got no idea what any of this amounts to. Before Kumu leaves today, we talk about our overlapping visits to Mt Shasta in a few weeks and make plans for connecting there.

**2021 Aug 8 - Dimensional experience -
Kumu's voicemail regarding the new
source of Light reaching our Solar System**

"A new source of Light is now reaching our
solar system, interpretating Earth's magnetic
field, altering the biological rhythms - this is
forcing the specie to leave behind its old time
cell of perception on the physical, emotional,
mental and spiritual level. This must take
place before the specie can go inside a new
time cell of consciousness with a unified
perception.

As the arcs of Light begin to change as
different light forces beginning to work with
the electromagnetic forces, this is causing the
magnetic fields of the brain cavity to be
sufficiently raised to a higher mental
frequency, allowing us to receive the whole

Light beings who will give instruction as to the program of the next level of creation.

It has previously been thought that the Light forces of the earth's magnetic field control the rhythms of life of all biological species and living cells need only the Light of our own portion of the electromagnetic spectrum to survive.

However, without new magnetic paradigms working with multiple arcs of color, the color of radiations of the Sun's light will not be sufficient for survival of the species.

We will therefore, begin to work with more of the complete spectrum major color factor, however it will be the warm white coating which will enable us to integrate with our original form sent from Higher Universe to this world."

2021 Aug 8 - Dimensional experience - QHHT session at Kathy's townhouse. Blue Cobra energy, Kathy's 'he's royalty ... he's a king' observation.

When I leave Mickey's on Sunday, I had reached out to Kathy, who is an Oracle in her own right. Her vocation had included emergency room nursing and now she administered a facility. Her real gift (and passion) is her ability to help others find past life connections using QHHT training. But Kathy's intuitive nature had already possessed these skills to deep dive because she is deeply empathic. I wanted her feedback on what had taken place and so she agreed that she would take me into a session and we would see what came of it.

I saw the Blue Cobra encircling me and posed facing me without fear of threat. It felt protective. That was all I saw. Kathy, however, came back with something more ... She saw something Egyptian

[She asked: "Who is Lowell?" ... she saw a sarcophagus tomb in shape of body ... leaning against the wall ... coming to life ... "Wake up" ... "Why Lowell?" The answers came back: He's royalty ... he's a king.

Cobra (for protection) Blue light ... light energy to use ... can direct that energy. Why the cobra ... grid in sacred geometry inside a square ... someone pulling on something around Lowell's heart and the cobra came forward and stopped it.]

2021 Aug - Dimensional experience - found the original Telos portal hiking with Christopher Rotolo

2021 Aug - Dimensional experience - Mount Shasta, CA Light being integration Kumu

That week before the conference went quickly like all timelines these days, toward the end of the week, Kumu and I had finally found a wedge of time early Friday afternoon to get to know one another better. I really knew little about her but I sensed she had something to give me and whatever it was I wanted it. But from where I sat at that moment and how things had assimilated ... it was clear that she had put me through ceremony without advising me that she was doing so, never mind without my consent. In the most respectful way possible I said she rather hijacked my Sovereignty and we had to overcome some trust obstacles. But whatever she was here to pass on to me I wasn't going to miss out on. She said she had to. I knew instinctively that she did, but I would have to spend a bit more time unlocking the reason why and it had to do with me, not her.

She then told me about herself – she is a hybrid and her history is not for me to tell, but I know she has dimensional connections, gifts and abilities beyond our current comprehension. She knows how to take the enhanced Photon Light energy pointed at the planet and transmute negative energy with the assistance of these higher Light Beings. She has been dealing with negative energies of unspecified kinds all her life and now it seems, others will be equipped accordingly to help clear. Somehow, maybe the day will come when I fully understand it all, she had to have received permission from a source higher than herself to share with me what I'm about to receive. I had no opportunity to ask anyone about any of this so of course I wanted to know "why me"? We went on to recognize all the things that had led to this moment and knew I had chosen it all. There were signs of things repeatedly placed in my path for weeks now on who I was, what I was here to do and this is where it started to come together. What we exchanged about me is very personal and so it won't be in print, those that need to know moving forward will – but opening that DNA with Etherium is about to be put to good use. Now Kumu had no way of knowing that I had been nourished by Etherium for months now, and in hindsight I believe it was preparing my being for more.

She held in her outstretched palms a red container. She said I was under no obligation to take what she offered me, but if I wished to deepen my connection to higher Light beings, this would help me get there. She said it contained Etherium … and … Light. Some I've shared my experience with asked "how could you ingest something you didn't know?" Admittedly, I never gave it a second thought when it comes to taking the concoction. My thinking was (and is) if I didn't take it – I'll never know what's in store for me. So over the next ten days, I ingested this sacred creation material and prepared to see what comes next.

Kumu invited me to a ceremony Friday night to participate in at a location in Mt Shasta with an energetic pyramid. There was unquestionably energy being shifted there that night and for me (after Kathy's Egyptian heads up), during the ceremony, I found myself at the Great Pyramid, where I removed its top ... giving access to the Halls of Amenti and the Akashic records for all humanity, including those Emerald Tablets which had been forbidden until now.

As much as I have been able to participate in some dimensional events that have resulted in showing me unusual phenomenon, magick can't really be anything but experienced.

Kumu was originally scheduled to leave first thing Saturday, but Friday night she invited me to one more ceremony and we would meet in town at Mt Shasta around noon to caravan to the site of the event. In all there were four vehicles and about a dozen people and I thought I was a tag along ... nooooo. Turns out – this ceremony was for me. I was to experience what this all had been leading up to – my Light Integration to connect me with higher dimensions and more specifically, these beings. In a later transmission I will tell you more about who they are but for now, know they are 6th dimensional beings primarily here to assist with ascension.

It took us about 40 minutes to reach the destination – a sculpture garden within a Veterans Memorial Park. Note: if you venture to see this space yourself, please be respectful of this location. It is sacred.

There is a rather circular drive where the sculptures are located so we all got the parking situated and then began to prepare the space for ceremony. I parked last and opened the back hatch waiting for further instruction. Kumu was on her way over to me while others were addressing the 4 directions to honor the space and ask to be granted passage.

When she came over to me she handed me a piece of brown paper and said "here is your medicine", take your chair and wait over by that statue until I come for you.

The weather couldn't have been more perfect. T-shirt temperatures and clear sun shiny skies. I found a spot with some shade, set up my star gazing chair and started taking in this medicine. It was just before 3PM when this candle was about to get lit. Kumu came over after all the other preparations were completed and her part of those were done. Now she was going to focus entirely on what was about to transpire with me. The energy was already elevated and so I was feelin' it already. She came over to where I was sitting to explain what I was to do. She pointed toward the sculpture in front of me ("Nurse") and said I'd be laying on my blanket underneath the statue and indicated how to position my head and feet. Then she asked me for MY iPhone so any images she might capture would be taken on my device. After I handed her my phone and I laid down, she told me to find my meditative state and ask what it is you want to know. I wanted to know about Thoth the Atlantean, his consciousness returning to assist Gaia and my role in all that. I said: if what I've been presented with is true, then let just one Light Being show as confirmation. What I received were Four Light Beings who made contact from their realm to this one with me and gave me some clarity regarding the Emerald Tablets and Crystal Skulls.

The encounter had to be quite the light show for mid afternoon on a Saturday. I could hear their vibration – three different instances that were confirmed by others where I heard high frequency vibrations, like a giant hummingbird hovering stationary over me while feeling a Light energy pulse upload to my system. More DNA activation was downloading into me while my entire energetic being was actually Integrating with these Beings. This is what REAL connectivity to All feels like. I now carry inside me the same DNA that these beings carry through the Etherium cocktail I had been nourished by. The die was already cast. These beings, call them angels if you wish, have always been around us assisting our oblivious selves, as they can without direct influence. Now however, a way to connect to this realm has been established to assist in the acclimation to use the higher enhanced Photon energy aimed at Earth to transmute negative energy into Light. Think of my connection as a dimensional "passing of the baton" and I'm not the only one – more are about to follow. That's my focus now moving forward: help others connect to this higher Light.

All of this happened one week before Rob's conference where I was expected to share the account of my visit to Telos (which we know most certainly now, was multidimensional). Very few people outside my immediate circle knew any of this had happened and as usual I was still making sense of it all. Do I mention the past weekend and the Light Activation or stick with the program and share Telos? It was decided to stay with our original presentation plan as many people with Lemurian / Telosian connections came to hear everything about that adventure. But by the end of the conference, I had shared with a few more insiders who I was comfortable having these conversations with and a buzz was starting to develop in the undercurrent. It wasn't just another story of someone's extraordinary contact, there were pictures of this connection as proof. And once again here I am after extraordinary events wondering – "Ok, now what do I do with what I know / can do?"

2021 Aug - Presented - Mt Shasta Summer Conference

My plans included presenting at Rob Potter's August Summit at the end of the month, but I would be going a week earlier to spend some quality "me" time on the mountain. Things always happen when I'm there now it seems and energetic signatures are more apparent.

2021 Aug - Project collaboration consideration, Justin West Assoc Producer, Discovery Plus

I was asked to consider participating in a program being produced for Discovery Plus about disappearances in the Mount Shasta area. The topic didn't resonate with me because my experiences were way beyond that, but I did refer him to Dianne Robbins and Rob Potter.

The beginning of September is getting busy with a few more interviews scheduled to bring a considerable amount of attention to my circumstances after the conference. There are also a few different production companies interested in different aspects of my experiences. There is one cord left to sever and that dissolves by the end of the month so I can focus entirely on whatever comes next.

I spent much of the first part of October catching up with tribe and sharing what had happened in Mt Shasta to keep them advised of changes in energy. The two interviews would be produced through Alan Steinfeld's NewRealities YouTube channel. After a few hours of Zoom time with Alan sharing my multidimensional experiences we came up with a two interview plan that would serve the Telos crowd and ease those who were ready into hearing such news that I've had a "different" kind of multidimensional contact with Higher Beings.

2021 Oct - Dimensional experience - marked location of Thoth's throne room entry to share with others, west side of Shastina, Mount Shasta, CA

I was instructed to show others this sacred area that has a portal to Thoth's throne room beneath Mount Shasta.

2021 Oct - Dimensional experience - Light being connection, ELEE OMs, Glass Mountain, Trinity-Shasta forest.

I spent the last two weeks in October receiving such preparations. I had commitments the first week that filled my dance card but the second week was for the mountain and I. Or so I thought. I spent everyday (Monday, Tuesday & Wednesday) on the mountain and activated additional energetic portals with Light from my integration. While I was going about this business and practicing the ELEE OMs I was given, the Light beings would show up to bridge between the dimensions and connect one with others (actual ascension). If your vibration is high and matching the frequency of the higher realms you are in alignment to experience such things now. You have been waiting to be activated in some way but didn't comprehend what that meant.

Because of my alignment, I had the opportunity to see Telosian Elders at a Lemurian Temple, during those three days. They are preparing for the imminent Shift and the reintegration of the cultures between surface humans and the Lemurians.

Monday, the most welcomed precipitation left the ground wet in town but the mountain was snow capped at that elevation and there was a cloud shroud hanging over her. My destination today was Glass Mountain – looking for a place of peace and solitude. The autumn colors added to the setting so I would be off to a quiet place to shout ELEE OMs today. I had no expectations for any contact, I was instructed to use these OMs to develop my own connection to these beings and those realms. After proper preparation and gratitude in these sacred settings they always show up now. My physical being is changing even more – adapting to the stasis (balance) that this state of consciousness awakens. Tuesday, I again spent solitary time at Bunny Flat and the snow atmosphere was blowing through regularly and saw an entirely new side of the mountain under pristine winter conditions. But Tuesday night I had little sleep as after another day with Light beings the evening would be filled with Akashic downloads that would last into the wee hours of Wednesday morning. When I looked in the mirror the next morning, the rapid download activity resulted in my right eye being largely bloodshot – but there was no pain, itching or discomfort of any kind. But some significant processing took place.

When I woke Thursday morning, physically and ethereally recharged, I wondered (again) "what do I do with this?". Two weeks earlier, Alan Steinfeld had asked me then, "what can you share with others to help them along their journey?". It was the second time Alan had posed a scenario to which I didn't have an immediate response – but one would be forthcoming. I knew I was here to help others but that can come in a myriad of ways. How do I leverage my Light connection for others? And within the last thought pattern was the answer with what I am now in a position to do. Leverage my connection to help others connect fully to the Light.

And that leads us to here: I have been given the tools and the authority to assist others to perfect their alignment, open themselves to greater capacities of Light and harness its power for your highest good and the highest good for All. It's all within you.

2021 Nov - Dimensional experience - Elementals, Enchanted Forest, Santa Cruz mountains behind Mickey Magic's compound

Upon instructions given to me by Kumu, I was to go into the forest and connect with the elementals ... did so in the Enchanted Forest behind Mickey Magic's compound and took pictures of Light emitting from inside a grandmother tree and pictures of sprites in the area.

2022 Jan - Collaboration project consideration NDA with Arjuna Somaru at Visionquest Management, LLC

2022 Feb - Dimensional experience - Spent last night clearing multiple beings and transmuting dark energy at John's compound, Santa Fe, NM

Santa Fe, NM
Spent last night clearing multiple beings and transmuting dark energy.
Nights at 7350' elevation get chilly.

After an evening of listening to experiences in this area that family have had, I picked up on the energies (more dark stood out than Light) ... there were many memories shared of experiences had with beings who would show themselves and then see how susceptible humans were to their suggestions and more dark were recalled than Light. There are plenty of reasons to understand why the conditions were right for dark energy to have grown here. All the more reason why its being unveiled now.

When I retired for the evening, it was chilly in this casa even with an electric heater and plenty of covers to bundle up in ... at this elevation, air is thinner and colder by nature, I was snuggling to get warm. I tend to sleep on my sides to get / stay warm and lay on my back once I need to cool off and balance.

There were only sheers on the windows so seeing the starry skies were possible from my perspective. When I first got into bed before the phenomenon began, I saw what I thought was a headlight shining just outside the window. It wouldn't take long to figure out it couldn't have been a headlight as we were too far away from both the road and the closest neighboring property.

The first time I found warmth on my back, I sensed a being within my orbit seeking Light to help clear the negative energy influencing him/her. In my mind's eye, I already anchored my Light and so I made it an intent to transmute any dark energy within my ethereal reach - into Light. It's what I can do now so why not put this mastery to good use?

I rolled over to begin again the warming up process now that I was getting chilly - as soon as I was warm enough to lay on my back again to cool - there waited another being who was seeking Light after being affected by dark energies that could use some assistance in healing beyond their own capacities.

By morning (7ish) upon reviewing the evening and the amount of rest my physicality really got - there was one being after another who during this warming process took advantage of energy shifts within my being to help clear blockages of their own. If I were to attach a number to it - 8 to 9 beings came to me this way and found the Light they needed to advance and clearing in this space took place.

2022 Jun 13 - Dimensional experience - Yedyamya transmission call - time to embody a Higher Self aspect who has been walking along side you, time to merge. You are the chosen.

L The last time we spoke, and you started to spew light language ...

Y *laughing*

L of course I want to go back to a time so I can process this, just like I've seen incredible artifacts that had codes on them that at some point I've been able to photograph. So later when I see them I can learn what it is that I was supposed to learn from it.

Y yeah

L Let's talk about you and how've you been. it's funny that you reached out now because of course we've been in touch with Lisa and Donald for a while. Stayed with them for a few days while we were in the area and then we had been talking about their interest in ayahuasca journeys and I'd had them ... It seemed as though their dots connected, because they just got back. I think the week before last from their own. And we were waiting until they assimilated it enough to share what had happened so ... the day after I spoke to them on the phone I'm sure that's when I got your email I went oh my God ... no no no I take that back because I made a point of telling Lisa - she had brought you up in the conversation for whatever reason and I don't know that you've reached out to her then I said you'll never believe it but I just heard from her yesterday and we're having a zoom session on Monday and something is going on. Anyway, it's just strange ...

Y *chuckles*

L how small the world gets right?

Y yeah well I'm, yeah Gosh, you know when we connected the first time I was on a bit of a walkabout.

L I remember that you were staying with Lisa for a day or so and you were just kind of in transition and so when she had shared our dialogue all of a sudden she reached out to me and goes. I have someone else. This is Cindy and so Cindy's gonna talk to you and then Cindy began speaking a language that I certainly didn't understand but I guess I'm supposed to. So anyway back to you. I won't interrupt anymore because I really want to serve whatever purpose we've got here today

Y yeah um ... so basically um i've been called to Mount Shasta you know and I've been hearing this call really strong so I'm hoping to leave by the end of this week but what I was told is that um very specifically very strongly to connect. We needed connect. You and I have an exchange. There's something I have for you (oof I got chills) something that you're holding in your field for me.
(more Star Language)

L I don't wanna interrupt but I want to get some clarity you said you're leaving for Shasta at the end of the week and how long are you gonna be there?

Y probably be up there a couple weeks

L what we're leaving for Shasta on the 20th

Y *giggles* uh huh

L we'll be there while you're there so we can connect physically while we're all there too but I definitely want to hear what's going on today

Y yeah they said my guide said that this was the first that we had to do this, so I imagine same for you. You need whatever you need for you before we get up there … ohhh I just got chills all over right now

L yeah so did I

Y um hmm So yeah, so there's something for us to receive now um and that I'm camping hopefully I've been given a very specific spot, not where I've ever been before to go camp. Oh, also before I do that, I have to go to Haruko's, and I have to go sit in the inner sanctum for a time to connect with the guardians that are holding that portal there. So um so that's what I've been told and it was like you need to connect with Lowell and I was like OK and then life goes on and I was just like doing my thing and I would hear you need to connect with Lowell and I go oh yeah yeah yeah I'll get to it I'll get to it you know and then it's like pushing pushing pushing and then I'm like oh you know I'm leaving soon, I better connect with Lowell so I'm glad we had the opportunity

L yes

Y so I'm just gonna um Well I wanna know how are you doing

L good

Y after all of this stuff

L it's it's assimilating and I know the cork is about the pop

Y yeah oof feel that

L The interview that I had started to do with Reuben Langdon, and the last episode of this season's interview with ED is me. It should've dropped by now in June and I was the last episode. But he's working on another project at the same time with Bill Homann and the Crystal skulls so for over a year he's been filming phenomenon as the skull has moved across the country and peoples experience with it. That has become a whole other documentary project. So he's at the same time, concluding that to turn it into a feature film, and still finishing producing the last episodes of you know his series. that's supposed to take place. There had been a guy up in Sacramento that is all about Lemurians and his channel Active Norcal and his podcast Talking NorCal about the Lemurians a lot. Well, I happen to notice one of his posts on YouTube that was talking about Lemurians and I left a comment saying that had a little bit of knowledge, and if he was interested in it, just reach out to me. And at first I'm sure he thought uh another crockpot. But something told him to follow up. Well I gave him the link to my blog and he read it. And he read it in detail. And it took him a long time to read it.

So he talked about it actually, they did a story on that article on his website. That was the year before last. It was the second most popular story they had all year long. So at the end of the year when they did their top 10 podcasts, this was number two. So they talked about OK we need to bring this guy onto the podcast so we've been going back-and-forth like this for almost a year and the last one was a little bit more um mindful and respectful, if we're going to bring this guy on, not to bring him up here and make fun of this. That we need to find a way to do this respectfully and he wanted to do it by zoom and I totally agree. Um, so we'll see. I'll bet that ... there was time this week - he's in Sacramento and I understand what he wants to do. So I had offered to come up one afternoon, let's have dinner, tonight and you get familiar - you can determine what I'm going to tell you is coming from a whack job or somebody that you know - isn't. And then the next day, we can do the podcast. We'll see how that shakes out. One of the things he has suggested is that he'd come to Shasta to do that and because of timing and as long as we're going to be there, that may end up how that's going to happen.

If that didn't get attention then I don't know what going to. But I say that - that was not my intent. Really I'd just as soon shut up and just serve my orbit. And never talk about this with anybody else. But that not the deal I signed up for. Was it?

Y right

L well that's my life

Y (more Star Language) I always say that my teams are opportunistic *laughs* because they come in just I mean in the grocery store, hiking, it doesn't matter where I'm at - it's just that if there's an opportunity we're here, so with that being said let's just see what wants to come in yeah?

L good

Y ok alright yeah so ah let's ground and let us just connect so let's close our eyes and just kinda take a couple deep breaths and bring your awareness inside and ah let's just connect our heart centers. Calling for our highest teams, our highest aspects, those that

have brought us together in this moment to be with us in a stronger way. Feeling that support of Gaia, felling that support of the cosmos
(more Star Language) so ah when the language comes through just - it's like it's like your ear is - like your body is an ear, let your whole body receive it without trying to just bring it through the mind.
(more Star Language) I was told there is going to be a big transmission today *chuckles* when we speak. My guides just told me that before we got on. So I've been called an Activator of the Activators so I don't know what will come through but I feel a - they want me to say that *chuckles* so just allow whatever comes through for you - you may start speaking or I don't know - you know Lowell remember the last time we connected I was having a huge process

L yeah

Y so yeah
(more Star Language) Mm they're telling me I've come a long way since then. Thank you. I also just returned from Egypt, I was with Lisa

and Donald in Egypt um doing the Matias thing and received a huge - I don't know whatever you want to call it - upgrade, embodiment, transformation ... so

L something was shifting there. Donald showed me some pictures that he had taken, that until he got back, he didn't really look very closely at them, and when you look at those, especially in the night sky, you see these strange curved patterns. Now they look like curved lights until you zoom in on them - it's a series of light dots in every one of the frames. So something's shifting over there, I'm not surprised you were there, we're all called to places we've been before and there's no doubt you've been there.

Y oh yeah yeah yeah, and I'm going back taking a group in March and friend and I are coordinating it. But um, my group, we were inside the King's chamber on Feb 22, 2022 at 3 o'clock in the morning. Yeah so that was a whole other thing. So I digress ...
(more Star Language) so in this moment I ask to be the clearest, purest channel possible to bring through the highest guidance and

healing for all of us gathered this day and that we may receive exactly what we need and require in this moment, for our highest good and potential and the highest good of all life.

(more Star Language) greetings

(more Star Language) so ask to be open for your cells, your body, your energy fields to receive what is being offered to you in this moment

(more Star Language) what is necessary

(more Star Language) for your um evolution, the next step

(more Star Language) ah Lowell it's like time for you to embody an aspect

(more Star Language) you could think of it like a higher self aspect

(more Star Language) it's like I feel like this energy has been walking with you so

(more Star Language) and now it's time to merge

(more Star Language) this aspect with you

(more Star Language) a higher version

(more Star Language) feels very tall

(more Star Language) um and he's asking do you feel, do you have an awareness of him are you aware of him?

L I know exactly what you're channeling

Y ok
(more Star Language) he's like saying my
brother
(more Star Language) it's time
(more Star Language) to walk in my shoes, to
walk this path
(more Star Language) what stops you from
believing in yourself
(more Star Language) do not resist emotion
(more Star Language) do not block
(more Star Language) the flow of energy
(more Star Language) coursing through you
(more Star Language) you are the chosen
(more Star Language)

L hold please

Y (more Star Language) did you have some
trauma in childhood

L ah not that I recall

Y beliefs but I mean like the beliefs that ah
(more Star Language)

L I'm going to tell you what this is about

Y ok

L it's hard for me to say the words because it's still fairytale-ish, and I knew at some point I was going to have to pull the trigger and just believe what I was told. Last year when I met Kumu, the hybrid I had my experience with and who put me in connection with the Light beings. I wanted to know at all that was about. Right before that, I'd been drawn to read the Emerald Tablets again ... try and understand it because in my first three passes at it - it was word salad but I knew I was interested in it and every time I heard Thoth, however you want to pronounce it - it resonated like hell will me. So when these things began to happen, when I finally got a chance to sit with her and find out who she was, we were in Shasta at Panther Meadows sitting at a campsite talking about that, I wanted to know why me and why these things were placed in my path. And in my wherewithal, I feel like I'm being prepared as a vessel to hold Thoth's consciousness when he returns

Y (more Star Language) this is what I bring to you
(more Star Language) this was downloaded to me in Egypt
(more Star Language)

L I'm not surprised that's where it took place

Y oooh (more Star Language) see I know exactly when it happened but I didn't know what it was but I know exactly when it happened

L I asked her while we were sitting there because after this conversation, she told me who she was, how she got there because I didn't know who she was before I met her and I didn't know anything about her but I knew she had something I wanted and I didn't know what it was - I just wanted it. So we got toward the end of our little conversation, I said so you're telling me that I'm being prepared to hold Thoth's consciousness and without hesitation she said - yes. You just have to believe that you are. We all hope that you will. And I just waited, I didn't know what

I was supposed to do with that - I didn't feel any different although I'd been having - I'd been ingesting Etherium since May until I met her - so she gave me some more Etherium that contained Light so for ten days I ceremonied and gave heated that. She had no idea that my body had been prepared to receive Etherium for the last five months before I even met her. How does all that happen and in my little 3D mind, how the hell do I comprehend any of that. And what everyone is suggesting and what you're here to validate today is still tough for my little 3D mind to believe - but that's what's taking place. I understand the importance of it all and who Thoth is and that's the part I have to let go of if this is all going to manifest the way it supposed to then I have to believe I in it and I'm still - it's not that I don't want to, I just don't know what to do with it once I do believe it.

Y you just have to be with it and to let it move through you. And I'll share this with you just because I understand ... I understand .. I understand. Ah and I've been embodying different aspects and like you know yesterday

Isis embodied in me so like yeah that happened. *laughs* but you know this is - we're avatars

L I get that

Y you know

L I totally get that

Y we are - we're avatars and you know we've been led to believe that this is all outside of us and we're these little you know unworthy little humans and all this other stuff that's beyond us but it's not. We're on the level, we're on the exact playing field you know. And we're here to remind everybody else that - the Gods on Earth.

L over the last couple weeks, more interest has been triggering inside of me to understand extraterrestrial roots - where I really came from, if I'm Pleaidian, then I really wanted to connect the dots. It wasn't that I hadn't had assistance with past life regressions getting me to see Atlantis, getting me to see Lemuria - got all that ok. Um but until Elysium was suggested from long ago, where that came from, how all that determined - I was on a tear the last two weeks to absorb as much information as I could to understand that. So I understand it for myself now what Elysium is and what surprised me is that what I carried away is we're so busy thinking that we're going from the 3rd dimension to the 5th dimension - that that's all our focus is. Well until I went back to study that information, Earth was a 7th dimensional being when she was created - and that is where we're trying to get back to. The Lemurians in their first incarnation were 7th dimensional androgynous beings, and until you really digest that, now you go whoa ... whoa - that's where we're trying to get back to. Not 5th dimensional consciousness, we're trying to rise the planet back to seventh. We came from the Seventh Galaxy of the Seventh Central Sun and we hold that sun disk in the middle of us. We come from the Sun of Illumination so all of the wisdom and how it generates itself came from where we were and that was planted in Inner Earth - here we are .. it's time for us to bring it back and humanity gets to finally get ... you know I struggle with the idea that we finally reach a level of consciousness we didn't before. And you wonder well the Atlanteans were 5th dimensional beings but they - would we consider that human? Well maybe ... that the part I struggle to understand. If we really ... if humanity is ascending to 5th dimensional awareness, and that level of consciousness and the claim is that humanity has never been there before well weren't the Atlanteans? So it doesn't matter whether I understand that or not, I know that we're going to a different place and that the Law of One prevails and we all know we're connected to one another - that's where New Earth is. So maybe we were having those thoughts while we were still planted on 3D earth and duality was still the rule of the day. But once her consciousness ascends, there's no more 3D planet to exist now. And we don't live in that world anymore.

Y no, my understanding is that it's not about humanity ascending, the earth is ascending, we are part of the earth - we are literally extensions of the earth

L correct - we're just sentient critters on her so when she ascends if our vibration is the same, I understand it exactly the same way

Y yeah I can definitely relate about trying to wrap the mind around the details and I think that's where we can get stuck

L we don't have the capacity to understand it

Y no *chuckles* that's what I've come to realize - you know what I stopped trying. I come from a very linear background, I need A + B to equal C. Otherwise, and you know now I just go whatever. It too me awhile to get thee you know but I get it I get it. So I think what my sense is, is that we needed this so you could *chuckles* marinate in what it is that's needing - it's really needing to happen, that you can make peace with it, wrap your head around it or not or just let it sit within your field so that you get used to the idea. And I think when you get to Shasta we need connect in person

L definitely definitely we'll do that

Y and let that be a ceremony, a sacred ceremony, because it's a right of passage and it's a great honor. Yeah?

L yeah I will have to let it sit and marinate for awhile. And it wasn't that I didn't do this after I first sat with Kumu last year, but as time's gone by, and things just feel like they're in neutral - um you kind of let it go and *chuckles* now that I see this instance right here ... I know I'm waiting for the time when something's going to come along to trigger it - hello Cindy ... thank you for calling

Y *laughs* you know I can say to you too that when you hear about, when you hear like this you know God is wanting to merge with you and become part of you um it's very overwhelming and you think you know I've gone through a lot of what does that mean for me and having embodied so many aspects for the past couple years what I've come to realize is - I just feel more and more like me. They're with me and as you see they flow in and out, honestly sometimes I don't even feel the transition, it's just all me. So I just want to share that with you because it's more about becoming more of who you are with that energy because it is a part of you or you wouldn't be the one to hold it. You know you are a part of that level. You get that - you're part of that soul field right?

L I do, I just have to be willing to embody it

Y yeah

L I've heard it and I think it's a cool idea but it isn't me right now and so that's kind of been my attitude

Y can I ask you is there any feelings of unworthiness like this is you know why me - no? Ok so

L I keep asking those questions and those haven't been satisfied yet but as of worthiness - no.

Y ok good

L that's not a concern for me at all, I know who I am and how special I am and I say that with the idea that so is everybody else.

Everybody is unique and gifted and is worthy
- we all just have different journeys

Y we do - so you can own your own worth?

L yes

Y and your value?

L yes

Y ok
(more Star Language) it is done

L I felt all that

Y whooo - like vibrating every cell

L somehow closing this with have a good day
really doesn't quite get it □

Y *laughs* I know right? I know I'm like peace
out. *laughing*

2022 Jun 16 - Dimensional experience - Mount Shasta, CA Thoth transmission Higher Aspect integration Yedyamya

https://youtu.be/iauou05U22g?si=r3iMrE46l XWA3ooO

Email from Yedyamya: I was just asked by Thoth to give you this message:
"Sunrise on Solstice, be on the mountain peak and wait for the call/instructions. You will be summoned at dawn." I asked what part of mountain did you need to go and was told, "He knows the location." I checked with my higher self to ensure the validity of message and it was confirmed, and that it was important to share with you asap.

Voicemail from Yedyamya: "hi lol this is Yedyamya or Starlight Cindy depending on who you know me from ... hey uh so I don't know if you got the email that I sent you with a message that I received from Thoth but I just got another one for you and this is what it says and i'm gonna ask you just to feel into the energy because maybe I didn't get every word specifically right because sometimes I get multiple words for the same you know they're trying to get the right meaning so anyways just feel into this he says tell him you are being summoned, we you await your presence at the portal the time is now delay not for what you are about to unveil is of the utmost importance for all humanity. It is time, it is time. Trust in yourself - not Lowell the personality but Lowell whose higher aspect Thoth is waiting for you. Trust you're all ready and release all expectations and perceived limitations. Allow your truth to be revealed and then that was the end of the transmission. So all right. I hope you're having a fantastic day. Happy trails, lots of love, bye."

2022 Jun 17 - Dimensional experience - Yedyamya Higher Aspect transmission

https://youtu.be/iauou05U22g?si=r3iMrE46l XWA30oO

Voicemail from Yedyamya: Star language transmission
"Who are you hiding from? This is the question to ask yourself. It's like moving past

the uncomfortableness. Not pushing through, but allowing it to move through you."

2022 Jun - Presented, led hikes - Mt Shasta Summer Conference
https://40kftview.com/hiking-to-energetic-portals-with-me-at-mt-shasta/

2022 Jun - Dimensional experience - Jami & Corey's, McCloud, CA Orb interaction, stayed in the dome

I had been fascinated with pictures of light orbs on Jami & Corey's property when she showed me pictures of her nieces surrounded by them. I would be invited to spend a few nights in a Yurt on her site and join others for an evening of Light orb interaction that would be photographed to share with others.

2022 Jul - Interview with E.D. Journey to Telos episode - then released on Gaia TV.

2022 Jul — Dimensional experience - Sam the Illusionist describes me by name during a Lemurian channeling for Adam Rykas, an Australian filmmaker traveling the world and capturing extraordinary phenomenon
https://40kftview.com/lemurian-feedback-lowell-johnson/

Sam the Illusionist channeling the Lemurians We are the Lemurians communicating now through the vibration system of this channel. We are now in communication from our location in the landmass referred to by your people and the language auditory sound system as Mount Shasta. Inside Mount Shasta we find our consciousness residing, and we are here to address an entity known as Adam, who desires to visit us inside Mount Shasta. We can already sense that this entities consciousness is pondering the thought of visiting us and has many times found itself doing so in the astral planes while using its imaginative body, therefore, we are now going to address the questions which are placed today before us. The first question that pertains to does Telos exist inside Mount Shasta? In this regard this we must state inside Mount Shasta there is a dimensional city, known as Telos however this requires the senses of inner awareness to be perceived, and sensed as the city known as Telos does not exist in the 3rd density reality. Therefore it may be difficult for entities in the form of human physical body to sense it with the five senses. Therefore we can state that Telos exists inside Mount Shasta. Furthermore, the other query which relates to is the entity as Adam able to visit it sometime next week. We must state that this visitation is permitted and also we must state that this entity can visit us anytime it desires, using its astral body which can sense our presence. This can be done by this entity, known as Adam while visiting inside Mount Shasta, which can be perceived by the senses of the 3rd density physical body.

Inside Mount Shasta it can enter into the silence within the mind, by keeping the inner vibration of its thought forms pure and empty. Thus will then provide it with the ability to sense our place of residence known as Telos which is created from a type of crystalline grid which may be harder to describe in your language as such objects and aspects of reality do not yet exist in the third density timeline. Furthermore the other query, which relates to what is it like over there. We must state that here there is only unity consciousness, peace, serenity, and positivity. The only aspect we have here, which is of value is our own consciousness. Much like many of the people on the Earth planet consider the so-called numbers on the screen as money to be valuable. We consider consciousness to be the most valuable aspects since without consciousness there cannot be any creation. In our social memory complex there are a total of 4.8 million beings who are primarily working for alignment of realizing the importance of space and time and the experience of reality creation is primarily the main objective for us to learn fully and to manipulate, love and compassion for such aspects. Our consciousness is also expanding rapidly. Our societal system primarily is consisting of entities from different levels of experiences who have graduated into the later fourth density and exist in the form of light body. For understanding how the system of inner vibration works, and the system of wisdom, which is to be learned at this time. Our society functions primarily on the basis of free will and love and unity and compassion.

The other query which relates to what type of technology do we use? In this aspect we must state that the type of technology which we have been using primarily consists of consciousness stream and reality of experience of consciousness. Furthermore the experience of mind body and spirit complex of the reality is to understand that all technology is created from consciousness. Without consciousness there cannot be any technological aspects. Our focus in understanding how our consciousness is a technological device is the main function of the reality of our work at this time inside Mount Shasta.

The other query which relates to any information about Lowell Johnson and how can he assist with ascension. The entity known as Lowell Johnson as we can sense is primarily trying to work for the attainment of more freedom in terms of consciousness and free will and has been in contact with us through its inner self many times since our vibrations match. It can assist in the ascension by transferring our information which primarily does not exist in the form of your language, but in the form of vibration, which can be transmitted and translated by its mind in a pure form for allowing the people of earth to understand fully our information much like this channel is performing, therefore we the Lemurians disconnect now bye.

2022 Aug 26 - Dimensional experience - Yedyamya transmission regarding connections between Peru (Lake Titicaca) and Mount Shasta and preparations for a mass activation

@38:38 Aramu Muru
- downloads flooded when your Andara was placed between your forehead and the appropriate spot on the stone

@39:33 Lake Titicaca
- around the Island of the Sun (long) with three smaller islands at the north end where they create a perfect triangle. Directly beneath that is a City of Light you can enter dimensionally. Took a boat to the center of the islands to connect the Light City below to the Light City above. Stabilized the pole of the Earth and stabilized the tectonic area specifically referred to as the navel of the Earth. Docked on one of the islands that was super sacred and climbed to the top, had a ceremony. Andara was gifted to the Shaman. From

Apu (mountain) Shasta. This expression connected the two areas.

@45:10 Asking to connect into the sacred City of Light within the waters of Lake Titicaca, nestled between these three power points

- 45:55 (I'm hearing Atlantean) counterpart to Telos - like they've been separated. We are reconnecting. Lowell representing Mount Shasta and that community of Light below - and Yeya above the waters of Lake Titicaca connected to the sacred city of Light - bridging the two. Ambassadors for each (energetic representatives holding the frequencies - grounding, earthing the frequencies into this physical reality - bridging the dimensional lines of Light into one unified network of the Inner Earth and above. To disseminate the information required. Uniting the elements of earth and water, air and fire allowing the transference of energy through the frequencies of water, the Record Keepers and the minerals, the Light holders, the memory recorders. Time for the memories in the water and the memories in crystal to merge, as if they're incomplete - separate and the merging creates a full record, a full picture.

@50:15 Time for each of you to fully embody your Higher Dimensional Aspect more fully in the physical

To gather your tribe for mass activation

2022 Sep - Dimensional experience - Yedyamya session, Thoth Higher Aspect integration

https://youtu.be/g9en47sm9y4?si=hXKBJ9th uy_seYvK

This is best experienced in the audio or video versions so you can hear and appreciate Star (Light) language. I am certain just hearing it will trigger something within you. But for purposes of this book - here is the transcript:

Y so let's see Like I said, I was ready to pop and then I just wrote I probably wrote like six pages but they were just nonstop which means something big is coming in It's just so massive that it can't be decoded.

L Do you need a moment to pull it together because I have something to offer you you had told me about when you started and it was a lot like Phil it sounds like when he began uttering late language. Well, let me tell you what the Lemurians told me last. Is that we are going to be the ones to help translate vibrations that aren't meant for humans to digest that way. You get it and that's the way that you translate it and overtime it becomes more refined. Well now is exactly when they said it's time for others to learn it too. So those that need to just hear it so that they understand it There's a whole other level of those that are also going to vibrate. Sam, the illusionist is one of those guys and the Lemurians are one of those entities he channels. but when he brought that through, especially in my regard. Through him, they had said it's time for humanity to understand this language. Now, you won't be able to understand it in your language because you don't speak that - it's in vibration. But these vessels they can translate it and help you understand it. So the time for you, and everyone else to refine that ability, here is why it's happening.

Y Yeah, it's definitely vibrational and that is why people resonate with it. I do know somebody who has been a shaman for like over 20 years and when I speak it, she can almost always decipher it. But she feels it. You know she'll tell you that have to feel it in your body and then she'll get the translation. As you know, I bring it through, but I don't always know what is being said.

L I do now.

Y I would probably say you don't always know though right? sometimes it's more of a feeling.

L I understand the vibrations. Every time I reflect back on hearing you, I can understand the nuances in between this one and that one. There's different patterns to it. I can put my finger on it. It's almost palpable, how do you do that with vibration and sound?

Y well cool

L There's very little of the comes through that I don't understand in my heart core. Now if you ask me, the interpret that into words, you can understand, I don't know that I have the capacity to do that - yet. I sense when there's information for me to "get", and then there's other information that's loving that we want you to understand. They're teaching you through that vessel. I get the differences.

Y yeah yeah yeah yeah. Sometimes when I'm bringing it through and usually when there's English and they're trying to get their point across like during a session for somebody, if that person's not getting it, they don't just go OK we'll go through another way, no no no, they push even harder and it feels like I'm up against a wall. I go, they're not getting it and I can't go any further because then it starts to get uncomfortable and then for me it sounds like it's coming out a bit snarky you know. But I think it's just the pressure that I'm feeling like I'm being pushed up against the wall because this person is completely resistant and um, so those are the only times that it's not fun.

L well, the day that I mentioned Thoth In the middle of our thing, and you kicked into a whole other level, that's when I got it. Because all of what led up to it was lovely to hear and yes, I get information, but as soon as I said that, it triggered something else.

Y yeah

L holy crap, I don't know what hit my ethereal field that day, but something did.

Y oh yeah yeah yeah yeah

L it was emotional

Y yeah and that's how for me even though I know that even if I'm not feeling anything during an exchange you know, if I'm hearing the language or whatever, and I'm not having any sense of anything. I know - something is going on still - right, that I'm not aware of. But it's those moments when I can feel it, that those are my favorite because it's just like wow you know, you just know ... so.

So I'm just gonna ask to ground. Ask to be the purest, clearest channel possible bringing through the highest wisdom, guidance and healing for Lowell, and myself in this moment, and the highest of all. And the highest love and light, peace,and truth and oneness and deep reverence for all life.

Y (Star Language) Greetings

(more Star Language) *chuckles* I'm hearing "greetings oh exalted one"
(more Star Language) my sense it that they are bringing codes to you
(more Star Language) I see like this something just dropped down through your channel

L laughing - I saw like an exclamation point

Y I saw something like this line in your channel
(more Star Language) You given yourself permission to receive?

L always open

Y (more Star Language) this is very important

L you're repeating it for me to get I see the patterns

Y (more Star Language)

L I feel like I'm a kindergarten and you're hammering it in

Y (more Star Language) so I'm just gonna ask is there something you're not getting?

L no, it's flowing

Y It's like I'm knocking it in

L it's emphasis that exactly what it is

Y (more Star Language) Making sure that it's being received all the way to the point that the layers ...
(more Star Language)

L Oh, it's so weird you said layers because that's what - when you were doing this before - that was layer one layer two followed then Layer three followed - your building this symbol that's all going to compress like a sigil and you tucked all that ina light package

Y (more Star Language) They're very happy with your progress that you can understand that
(more Star Language) bring your awareness into your throat
(more Star Language) They're planting a seed

(more Star Language) Breathing into the throat
(more Star Language) Breathing into the seed
(more Star Language) when it's time it will sprout
(more Star Language) It will blossom
(more Star Language) this time is not now
(more Star Language) There is many things that need to happen before this comes to fruition
(more Star Language) You must embody more
(more Star Language) More of your essence
(more Star Language) bringing it into the physical vessel
(more Star Language) Saturating yourself
(more Star Language) It like feels like ah for lack of a better word - upgrade
(more Star Language) That's needed for your cellular structures and the organisms within the cells to hold more light

L the metamorphosis you referred to

Y holding higher frequencies
(more Star Language)

L Yeah, you tucked it in. When you went like this, you buried that in my hard-core, then you brought out that seed that you planted here so whatever this is going to hatch you planted here prior

Y (more Star Language) So they want to bring through some recoding
(more Star Language) see this *chuckles*
(more Star Language) recoding
(more Star Language) recoding
(more Star Language) recoding
(more Star Language) they're going to pause for a moment

L good and I'll tell you why. I was just listening to you flow and tucking it away, like I have in the past when I didn't understand what you were telling me, because the whole time you're doing that my lower jaw vibrating, and if I brought my mouth close enough, my teeth would chatter. so I am trying to keep them separated but while you were channeling all that I am focusing on the physicality, so you recoding go ahead and do because I can't get past the fact that my jaw won't stop vibrating

Y (more Star Language) it's cellular recoding

L I ... ohhhh ... wow ... ok

Y (more Star Language)

L it was palpable pal

Y thank you for the confirmation. So I just need to confer with them for a moment. (more Star Language)

L Wasn't like I hadn't been asking for this freaking upgrade for a while

Y *chuckles* ok

L bring it, you want me to embody this - help me

Y well, I'll share with you this week, right I received all this stuff that it's time to recode the human genome, um it's time to do an at level that's never been accomplished before, and this is something that they want me to do and I was like ah this sounds like a bit too much for me in this moment to take in and you need to confirm this with me in someway that's that I haven't solicited somebody like can you confirm this I need confirmation and they told me - Lowell and they didn't say anything else.

L *laughs*

Y and I said OK well in my mind, then you're going to bring that up somehow like maybe you're gonna pick up that I need, that it's time to start recording. This is what's happening, they want to recode the DNA and RNA so that it can hold more light. It's basically the (more Star Language) like um, recoding, or um reworking it because it's been manipulated yeah, our DNA's been manipulated and um

L all the more reason why like the day before yesterday I pushed Kumu's thing about Light out again

Y ah

L to think about that again and I guess it was a reminder for me too. Yeah let's go back to that I'm fully aware of the photon light energy that we're getting right now and it's enhancements and I sense it when it happens when we get these solar phenomenon - Yesterday was interesting, riding an earthquake. That was fun.

Y did you have an earthquake

L oh yeah honey a 3.4 - 3 km north of my location here was the epicenter. Now that hasn't happened in Santa Rosa in I can't tell you how long. It's just more manifestations. Here's your physical proof that earth is flexing and getting ready for the next thing.

Y (more Star Language) So they're just making me feel images of the cell
(more Star Language) And like um, distorted DNA being removed
(more Star Language) and the new DNA or the, I don't know if you wanna call it new because it's not new, it was our original design is what I feel being returned

(more Star Language) this takes - this is what they were telling me before. It's like a series of five. It's a process of five layers, right (more Star Language) OK so now it feels like another group coming in that are geneticists (more Star Language) They feel very different (more Star Language) Just wanna make sure these are the highest (more Star Language) Highest levels here (more Star Language) Their energy just feels really different

L they're geneticists

Y I know, but still, I'm just like, just always pause and go. I just wanna make sure that we're good. These are the best, this is the beat team that we have (more Star Language) I feel like my head really long and I'm tall

L More dots connect we do these types of things you know when we get those sounds in our ears, that ringing, I understood that my left ear implies that I'm getting spiritual downloads and I get those often, I haven't had them for a while because I think I got what I was supposed to get. I understood that the physical ones were my right ear. And I didn't really understand what that meant for what I should feel.. but today I get it. I finally got it because the whole time we're having this session the back of my neck is getting stiff and across the top of my shoulders. so that cellular change that you were talking about yeah it's freaking manifesting itself physically. And so you said the geneticists are here I was gonna say, can you ask them to do something about that thing in the back of my neck while we're at it? Because I physically feel it, I feel like my head is heavier, and it takes more effort to have my neck hold it up.

Y I don't think it'll stay that way
(more Star Language) Make yourself as comfortable as possible
(more Star Language) Try not to put too much attention to it
(more Star Language) They suggesting to put your attention into your feet on the ground. They always have me come to the bottom of my feet, and really put my attention there. So really coming into the feel of the bottom of

my feet, can I feel it? What does it feel like -
bottom of my feet, bottom of my feet, bottom
of my feet
(more Star Language) and now I'm getting
this (gestures upward winding columns)
(more Star Language) they're telling me they
just want to bring it through and for me to
stop trying to understand what I'm doing
while I'm doing it, it's fascinating

Both laugh

L we're humans that's why I keep
commenting on the physicalities because I've
never had the opportunity to express it and I
feel the things that you're trying to tell me.
And so when I'm going to explain it to others -
because I feel there's going to be the need to
do that later I have to put it in terms that they
can understand too and yeah we're physical,
these are carbon bodies, and there's a feeling
that comes associated with these things that
have been this nebulous idea about changes
in our DNA and physicality - that whole
process from carbon to crystalline, here your
activating part of that with what we're doing
here

Y yes more - activating more of it because it's already been started yes

L correct

Y (more Star Language) they're asking me to step aside a little bit more

L *laughing* whispers - we're trying to understand it

Y they're saying it's recorded so you can go back and listen

L *laughing* Who said spirit doesn't have a sense of humor

Y oh yeah they definitely do but the humor is what helps me out of letting them in fully because it's so physical you know the feeling of especially when I laugh it's very physical and I'll tell you a story story about that another time

L ok

Y (more Star Language) So they're showing me like preparing you for surgery
(more Star Language) just remain still as you can, and relax as much as possible
(more Star Language) the team is tending to you
(more Star Language) We are experts
(more Star Language)

L I see them around me having this conversation

Y (more Star Language) They know you
(more Star Language) They're saying it's good to be with you again
(more Star Language) Though your form is different
(more Star Language) Your energy is the same
(more Star Language) And there is recognition.
(more Star Language) They're thanking you for volunteering for this

L I'm grateful it's them

Y As they do this, somebody else is going to come in
(more Star Language) so they step aside
(more Star Language) They're telling me to ground which doesn't usually happen so I'm assuming this is a big energy.
(more Star Language) Greetings and they said a name, but I don't know what the name was
(more Star Language) [integration process] Beloved one
(more Star Language) Thoth is not the only aspect of you
(more Star Language) seeking to reconnect
(more Star Language)

L *laughing in amazement*

Y (more Star Language) you are
(more Star Language) also
(more Star Language) a great commander
(more Star Language) aboard one of the motherships
(more Star Language) This is how we know each other
(more Star Language) My aspect is a high commander
(more Star Language) see we are equals

(more Star Language) ah comrades
(more Star Language) You may feel yourself traveling
(more Star Language) Great explorer of the universe
(more Star Language) Record keeper
(more Star Language) your world is about to blow open
(more Star Language) important to anchor
(more Star Language) or you'll get swept away
(more Star Language) You're receiving information at night
(more Star Language) about the nature of the galaxy
(more Star Language) black holes
(more Star Language) traveling through Black holes
(more Star Language) complexities
(more Star Language) of the universe
(more Star Language) many more will be seeking you out
(more Star Language) to speak of Galactic things, of cosmic things that which is unknown to most of your population
(more Star Language) You will be branching out

(more Star Language) More to be revealed
(more Star Language) so they're making me feel this and this is what I was telling you before you gotta be able to if someone does a name search on you that goes to your website you gotta make sure that you're easily found (more Star Language) it's not about driving traffic to you. It's about driving people to you who are seeking answers.
(more Star Language) making it a little bit easier for them
(more Star Language) because not many are capable of um Internet, detection, or Internet detective work or something
(more Star Language) because you are a connector and you wanna make it easier for people to connect with you
(more Star Language)

L I do however, I feel like it has to be an organic process and if I feel like I tried to manipulate it …

Y you're not manipulating it you're not manipulating it. You're just making it you're just putting it. However you do it. When they

Google your name automatically popped up your website but right now it doesn't right? (more Star Language)

L no, it does not at all

Y it's not about making them find you. It's about when they hear you they google you that's what everybody does now but it's not easy for them to get you right now and more people are going to want to interview you and speak to you because that's important. Then you are getting into their audience, so everyone has their own little audience. It's about bringing them all together.
(more Star Language) shared knowledge (more Star Language) that it's all connected - every part that everyone is learning that everyone is learning an individual and is actually all connected and it's about connecting all of it into into one hub that people come to to find out about all of this stuff it's a bit like

L agreed

Y (more Star Language) because it goes way beyond Mount Shasta and your experience in Telos
(more Star Language)

L that's the shiny disco ball to get your attention

Y (more Star Language) but that did a lot for your own awakening because being down there actually recoded you - and put stuff into your field which is what I picked up on the first couple times we had an exchange
(more Star Language) so they're saying don't dis- I don't wanna put words in your mouth but what I'm feeling is this - don't discount the experience, don't make it just be like that was this one little thing

L oh no I elaborate, but I understand the bigger picture so when I speak now it from that perspective that I see the bigger picture - this is about multidimensionality - that's one piece

Y (more Star Language) I do you feel like you'll be going back

(more Star Language) I don't see you taking a group of people in there but I do see you going back
(more Star Language) because there's more, more to be shared
(more Star Language) so my sense is that whatever they were doing as far as like the surgical team that is coming to an end or it has already ended

L it's already ended

Y so you are in a bit of the recovery state

L It has already ended

Y (more Star Language)

L do you want my perception of what just happened

Y sure

L yeah, when my expert buddies stepped off to the side and that other entity moved forward - that was Thoth. It was like he was taking the driver seat. He was being embedded because I've been asking for this - you said that this was going to happen and that happened. So when that was in place, there was a surge of energy that went through me while you were saying that and at the same time it was like he was leaving space for another aspect and as soon as that came into my head - you said what you said

Y *laughs* sweet
(more Star Language) because it's about it's it's about bringing the fullness of our soul field or our oversoul into our awareness but into the physical right and so there's many aspects of that. That's awesome.

L and by the way ... the stiffness in my neck - gone.

Y perfect
(more Star Language)

L so whatever they did that created a little trauma at the beginning it's been relieved

Y feels it was a stabilizer, some sort of stabilizer to stabilize you physically

(more Star Language)

L ok

Y I was like whooo - I just have like the
biggest hair-raising on the back of my neck -
so
(more Star Language)

L this wasn't like putting on a shirt, this was
like I got embodied from the inside out and
like I feel like I'm armored here

Y yes

L it wasn't anything that I applied from
outside

Y no no no
(more Star Language) it should always come
from the inside
(more Star Language) so you're going to want
to give yourself some downtime. Just you
know, just let the body catch up to the higher
frequencies right
(more Star Language) also the cellular
restructuring

(more Star Language)

L I feel that taking place. I look for the physical stuff now. I got my spiritual downloads and I know that I benefit from those but I was always trying to associate when my right ear goes off, where's the physical part I was led to believe was being altered. Well now, little empath, now you get to feel it. When I wanted my empathic skills back, it was because I envied somebody who could pick up a crystal and feel its energy. And so that's what I wanted more than anything, I didn't have that. Well when you get that back, it's not just crystals you're going to be able to sense - you asked for it, you get it all. So you'll sense changes not just in you, you sense them in the people around you and when you allow that energy to come in, then I can translate it for them too. But yeah I don't like it - the first time it ever happened was with Paul of Venus and it wasn't a pleasant experience because he was describing getting electrocuted on stage. Yeah I'm very careful and maybe they set me up as a learning lesson that was gonna be my first experience.

Y yeah but you can choose, you can choose what you want to feel.

L *laughing* I ahhh, yes but I didn't have that mastered the first time around

Y oh yeah yeah yeah I get it. Believe me I get it

L learning curve

Y *laughs*
(more Star Language) they're telling me that your empathic skills are actually quite sensitive and that this is - it's helpful for that to be so sensitive because you are able to help people understand what they are going through that I've shut it down.

L yeah I know - I still cry watching America's Got Talent so tell me how sensitive I am

Y yeah I'm right there with you I can totally relate
(more Star Language)

2022 Sep - Dimensional experience - Inner Earth related AI images begin pouring out of me.

The Halls of Amenti: Home of the Akashic Records

The past ten days or so showed me the reach of my accounts and where reports of them are showing up. TikTok, Rumble and Bitchute are a few channels I have no experience with and yet, links to the discussions of my Telos adventure on the ActiveNorcal podcast can apparently be found there. It was there that JimBob from the Unconstitutional Awareness podcast found said story. He has a soft spot for Mt Shasta like many others and he reached out to me to see if I'd be interested in sitting down for a session with him and his sidekicks Luis and Bandit.

As is the experience I always have, there is something meant for me in these exchanges as well. This was going to be no exception. Toward the end of the podcast, Luis who is a talented graphic master started to show me some of his work specifically some visions he had of Telos. I have said for sometime now, I wish it was possible to pull in video form the movie of my experience inside Mt Shasta out of my head so that the rest of you could see it like putting on an VR headset. When I saw some of his work, it occurred to me that here may be someone who could take my vision and illustrate it to share with others. I see us collaborating on a project like this down the road, but there was an attention getter about to trigger me with something I was about to see toward the end of his presentation.

Luis in the end, wouldn't be the one who would channel these images for me - no. He would point me in the right direction to able to do it for myself to share with others. Eventually, these images as they triggered so many others, will be produced in four different categories (Inner Earth, Stargates and Portals, Galactic Travelers and Elementals) in coffee table book form, affirmation card decks and used in videos illustrating Inner Earth cities.

2022 Sep - Earthquake - Home, Santa Rosa, CA

2022 Oct - Presented - GSIC Conference - Orlando, FL

Presented my Light being experience with images to show what happened to an audience of about 1000.

2023 Mar - Inner Earth collaboration project - Berlin

2023 May - Dimensional experience - found a Golden Taya vortex in Mt Shasta on private property, set a spiral
https://youtu.be/Z7ydz1qawfM?si=TzhfTsDJHvR25tK-

What are Golden Taya allotments

"This information has made its way to humanity through the steadfast work of Maia Nartoomid @ newearthstar.org. Her body of work has created a vast archive of the work of Thoth (and much more) since the mid-70's. It's no coincidence that this information is surfacing now as we can all sense that the Shift Earth's consciousness has been moving toward is upon us and the wisdom Thoth channeled through Maia is about to be put to good use – if you are paying attention that is …" What follows is from a 1995 channeling.

The Golden Taya Allotments are the areas of Earth's surface which will be ascending through the veil into the fifth dimension at the period of time referred to as Light Principle 40 (LP-40) by Tehuti/Thoth and his Merkabah group "Chariot of the Sun".

According to Tehuti, the currently projected occurrence of LP-40 will fall somewhere between the years 2015 and 2025.

On February 17, 1995 we were experiencing some very powerful, yet strange dynamics. This prompted us to go to Tehuti and ask what was going on, as there seemed to be an unidentifiable component in the energy we were experiencing that day. Tehuti replied that this was the first day of the 'passing of the guard' of some of the Golden Taya areas from the control of the fallen lords (Nephilim) of light to the true Lords of Light (Solarians). He indicated this process would be occurring until approximately March 12, 1995 for the initial 20% of the Golden Taya Allotments.

As Tehuti had mentioned the Golden Taya in 1981, and now here they were again, we felt it important to ask some additional questions regarding the Golden Taya's purpose, history and dynamics. The results were quite revealing and we will present them in the question and answer format the information was transmitted through in an effort to maintain as much of the original vibration as possible.

Maia: Can you give us some history on the selection of the Golden Taya allotments, who was involved in the decisions as to what was to be considered Golden Taya, when did this occur?

TEHUTI: Those whom we call the Sun Bow Clan, also know as the Kachina (of the Hopi prophecy) were responsible for these decisions. They were master builders sent from the confederation of stars known as Orion, but primarily they came from the blue star "Rigel". This occurred after the first fall of Heaven, prior to the end of the Hyperborean Epoch which resulted in the ascension of a portion of Atlantis known as the "Holy Isle of Ruta" at the final cataclysm that destroyed the remaining continent. The Sun Bow was assigned by the Ennead (Council of Nine Seraphimic Intelligences, more information available) to determine the present-future consciousness vectors of Earth, and assign Light ascension matrices for specific sacred land areas under the Mandate of the Violet

Flame. It was understood that not all of the Earth would be viable for translation at the time of LP-40. The regions containing certain Light Codes were those appropriated back to the Metatronic Full Light spiral at the time of ascension. The rest of the Earth would be given up to the entropy of the fallen elements.

Maia: On February 17, 1995 you indicated to us that a "passing of the guard" had occurred. Please elaborate further on the dynamics of this changeover, the history of the agreements made between the Nephilim and the Solarians and the subsequent reprogramming of all matter within the Golden Taya.

TEHUTI: The Earth was designed as an outlet for karmic pathing (evolution towards Grace). It was decreed by the Archangels of the "Seventh Heaven" (Seraphim, Cherubim and Wheels of Fire) that a mandate should be established for this return to Grace which the universes were moving through. You must understand that the Earth's plight is of an inner design as part of a greater universal "return home". The universal mandate is that of the Violet Flame. The Earth's role is given several sub-mandates under the Violet Flame. One of these mandates is the Golden Taya, which concerns the allotment of certain light encoded areas for the LP-40 ascension. The first step in this process involves their transfer from Nephilimic guardianship to Solarian guardianship under the authority of the "Wheels of Fire" containing various Merkabah groups such as "Chariot of the Sun".

At the time of the Earth's creation it was known that the fallen lords (Angels of Lucifer), including the incarnating Nephilim, would enter the Earth's spectrum and claim guardianship over its basest elemental state. This was allowed by the God Source as part of a larger process designed to create separation in order to redesign the fragments of Self back into unity. Within the Mandate of the Violet Flame the fallen ones could not lay claim to anything but the basest elemental state. The higher regions, including the Metatronic Gate would remain within the guardianship of the Solarians. It was determined within the sub-mandate of the Golden Taya guardianship that even the elemental substance known as your world would be turned over to the Solarians prior to LP-40 ascension. This must be accomplished in order for these Golden Taya areas to ascend through this gate, 20% of the Golden Taya must have their guardianship transferred prior to the Light schematic of the Emerald Pyramid being relinked to the other six Holy Doma Pyramids. This latter activation occurring March 12, 1995 through July 15, 1995 (more info available). The transfer of guardianship is a process encompassing many levels of being, requiring cooperation from the nature Devas to the high Angelic dominions.

From March 4-11, 1995 the Devic kingdom in the Golden Taya lands in which the guardianship is being transferred will experience a "rush" of Metatronic Light programming energy into the soil, rocks, crystals and plants from within the center of the Earth. This will later be absorbed by animals and humans. The Inner Earth realm is more engendered with this Light potential than the surface. The Earth's true program for ascension lies within a crystalline plate, the innermost layer of the ice canopy near the central sun of the planet. This plate is called the Korpala and projects a natural hologram into the center of the central sun atoma. This in turn sends a signal or directional beam through the time continuum (Ranna Time Wave, more info available) connecting the second millennium (current consciousness) to its pathing towards the third millennium (Future consciousness). The Korpala was inserted into the ice canopy by the Sun Bow Clan. All soil, rock, crystal and plant forms within these initial 20% of the Golden Taya are receiving their "Doctrine of Signature" (etheric Light body programming) for the New Earth Star reality. This will not be detectable until the growing season is underway, at which time a new etheric presence will manifest in the living Earth of these ascension regions. Each new bud will be awakening from its sleep into a new consciousness full of Light beingness. This will be the beginning of the time when the Unicorn returns.

The physical manifestation of this new programming will be a gradual unfolding process. Weather will become more stable and less differential in these areas, although at first some of these regions will experience clearings requiring more severe climatic changes and some cataclysmic activity. One such area is the Salt Lake Basin and the surrounding Wasatch mountain range. Although this is a Golden Taya and the future location of a Holy City, it will have to undergo a massive cleansing before this can take place. This area is not among the first 20% of the Golden Taya returned in guardianship to the Solarians. When Angelic guardianship is resumed in the near future this region will experience upheavals as part of its ascension preparations.

Maia: Please give some clear information regarding the role of the Golden Taya in the planetary ascension process, and are they the same as the major ascension centers of the planet?

TEHUTI: The Golden Taya are the major ascension centers of the planet, and the only areas so designated. There are areas such as the "Valley of the Golden Disc"(Crestone – San

Luis Valley, Colorado) that are major activators of this energetic, but all Golden Taya are equal in the degree of ascension they will assume. This is necessary in order for them to merge into the New Earth Star World. However, all Golden Taya areas will not ascend within the same moment. The entire process for both land areas and Souls upon them will continue for 15 days in linear Earth time of that age.

The Golden Taya are the physical Earth upon which the New Earth Star will be designed. They are like seeds containing the memory of the God Self and the "return" program that is the software for the new matrix of consciousness.

Maia: Please explain how the Golden Taya allotments will be able to ascend through the veil at LP-40 prior to the rest of the planet, and will those outside of these areas be able to ascend as easily as those within them?

TEHUTI: Only the Golden Taya, the incarnated and disincarnated Souls gathered upon these areas, at the appointed time, will ascend through the veil. The remaining planetary Earth and its Souls will face the final chaos being absorbed into the evolutionary cycle once again. These souls will be given a new beginning point on another planet, starting once again up the ladder of Spirit. Do not fear that some souls will be left out of the ascension simply because they are not in the right place at the right time. All souls in that period will be under the Violet Flame Mandate. If that Soul's Higher Self has chosen the ascension, they will be where they need to for that process. Ironically, there will be many Souls who will rush to the Golden Taya out of fear, feeling drawn to a "safe" place, only to become disillusioned and fearful of the challenges in releasing their elemental magnetics. They will then leave these areas before the ascension time. The gatherings of Souls who have chosen ascension as their path rather than returning to the Oritronic half Light Spiral in another planetary realm, are what we refer to as the Anubis Gatherings.

It is important to understand that there is another form of ascension which is ongoing to this time on the planet. This is what we call the Heart ascension. It is the raising of ones Heart consciousness vibration, which in graduated levels is freeing individuals from the entropy of their fears and illusions. This form of ascension is of absolute necessity in order to achieve the full transcendence of LP-40.

Maia: Could you give some examples of the Golden Taya Allotments and their approximate boundaries? Are they triangular in shape?

TEHUTI: The Golden Taya represents in all, 20% of the Earth's surface area (nearly all of the inner Earth will ascend). As we have stated before, we anticipate that approximately 40% of the souls incarnated at the time will choose ascension. This is a choice made at the level of the Higher Self of the Soul. There will also be disincarnates who have not yet lifted through the veil who will choose to ascend, and some will not. Also, there are those Souls already in the higher spiritual Heavens who will choose to reincarnate in the Metatronic body of the New Earth Star, and others whom will not be free of the magnetics of the incarnating cycle of the Oritronic half Light Spectrum, returning to the lower physical once again in other planetary worlds.

The physical shape of the Golden Taya differ vastly. Their size does not conform to any specifics. Some of the Golden Taya are as small as three to five acres while others encompass many hundreds of miles. We will give a few of the ascension lands here in approximation only:

- Grand Tetons, Wyoming
- Sedona / Mogollon Rim, Arizona
- Mt. Shasta, California
- Klamath Lake, Oregon
- Crestone / Baca / San Luis Valley
- Zion National Park, Utah
- Much of the British Isles
- A major section of Iceland
- A section of Greenland
- Many small but potent sections of Egypt
- Rennes Le Chateau, Southern France
- The Tibetan Himalaya
- Mt. Arat region, Turkey
- Portions of Greece

- Most of the Hawaiian Islands, including some now below the water

The sacred geometry of these regions, when translated onto a spiritual-elemental map are triangular in nature, but not in arrangement of their spatial dimension in the present Earth reality. Some of the Golden Taya will experience significant reshaping through cataclysm before LP-40 ascension.

Maia: Do all the Golden Taya link to form a large Temple structure, or are they simply nodal points connected on a grid?

TEHUTI: Yes, these lands form the Grand Templaric. Their etheric counterpart is the Templa Mar complex (more info available). The "Valley of the Golden Disc" (Crestone/Baca/San Luis Valley) assumes the Crown center of the Golden Taya Temple. We now give you a listing (at Maia's request) of the major chakra centers as they correlate to the Golden Taya Ascension Temple.

- 1st) Base or Kundalini Center: The Hawaiian Islands, center point being the large Island, Hawaii. This is what we call the Roil point of the present Earth. With the pole shift the Roil point Becomes Rennes Le Chateau, France (more info available)

- 2nd) Navel Center: Rennes Le Chateau region, France, center point being the seed chamber (see "Genesis-The First Book of Revelations" by David Wood for approximation of seed chamber location.
- 3rd) Solar Plexus Center: Sedona/Mogollon Rim region, Arizona, center point of the Mogollon Rim.
- 4th) Heart Center: Grand Tetons region, Wyoming, center point within the Tetons.
- 5th) Throat Center: Ayers Rock region, Australia, centre point Ayers Rock.
- 6th) Brow Center: Glastonbury "Crystal Isle" region of England, center point Tor Hill.
- 7th) Crown Center: San Luis Valley, Colorado, center point Crestone/Baca

Two more chakra centers (and thus Ascension Gates) will open for the Earth just prior to LP-40. These are the two Metatronic Pillars named here as Osiris and Isis.

- 8th) Osiris Center: Dead Sea/Mt. Sinai region of the Middle East, center point near the Dead Sea
- 9th) Isis Center: Easter Island region of the Pacific Ocean, center point Easter Island

There are three more Ascension Gates oriented to the "Capstone" of the Metatronic Temple.

- 10th) Sheba Gate: Ethiopia, a region not far from Addis Abeba, center point not clearly defined on a map.
- 11th) Thunderbird Gate: Alaska, region of Denali and Matanuska Valley, center point Danali (Mt. McKinley).
- 12th) Zion Gate: Zion National Park region of Utah, center point, The Great White Throne.

It is important to understand that these areas perform specific grid functions for the entire Golden Taya ascension dynamic. At the time of LP-40, a Soul in one of these regions listed as Ascension Gates will not be more ascended than a Soul in any other Golden Taya area. Souls in the Ascension Gate areas will, however, undergo specific experiences unique to that Gates function prior to LP-40 and during the LP-40 "lifting" process.

Maia: Can you give us some information on the specific function of the Crestone/ San Luis Valley Crown Gate and what we might experience here as an example of what these specific functions and experiences might be?

TEHUTI: The Crown Gate serves as a meeting point between Human and Devic experience both merging with Angelic consciousness bringing these threefold into an experiential reality. This will be a place of transformation for many back into their original-future physical forms through their Sunoma bloodlines (more information available). Many humans will be drawn here to transmorph into their fairy/elfin bodies or variations thereof. A strong connection will develop between the Valley of the Golden Disc and both Tibet and Great Britain. The Masters and high Devas from these two other planetary regions will merge with the consciousness fields unfolding in the Golden Disc area. The Tibetan connection is already very strong, with the Celtic/Devic soon to be manifesting more strongly through the "Dream Corridor" established by the Native Americans. The Crown Gate is the place of Devic/Angelic infusion through the sacred blood energetic into the physical elementation.

Maia: Are there any procedures that individuals living within the Golden Taya areas can utilize to facilitate the higher etheric work being done to prepare these areas for LP-40 or to link the vibration of that area to others?

TEHUTI: Souls in the Golden Taya regions would do best to focus primarily on their Heart ascension and enjoin this personal energetic with those in their immediate consciousness field. There will be certain Light Workers within these Golden Sections that will be called upon to perform specific functions such as anchoring Templa Mar grids, Earth healing, etc.

Linking with other areas would fall within whatever specific Light service was being given. It would be difficult to correctly give an overall outline for this work as each Golden Taya area calls forth different functions and directives. Many Souls will enter these Golden Taya Allotments with their main purpose being to anchor Metatronic Light there.

Maia: Would it be appropriate for the Souls now consciously anchoring Light in these area to leave the areas for any prolonged period of time?

TEHUTI: They should be selective in their trips outside of these regions, but often it may be part of their function to connect that particular Light encoding with other regions and Souls. It would be best that journey outside the Golden Taya region be for specific Light work.

Maia: About a year ago, you gave the projected time frame of LP-40 to be between the years 2015-2025, does this still appear to be accurate, and what are the best avenues for individual Souls to assist the acceleration of this time frame?

TEHUTI: The projected time frame of 2015-2025 is a loose projection only. As the ascension vehicle is built from the components of Spirit within the planetary world of consciousness evolving along its return to the stars, this window could well move forward or back in time. It is true that we are not giving definitive information on this timetable as we do not wish this information to be inserted into the planetary consciousness at this time. Such an event may limit the co-creative participation of the Souls involved.

The acceleration of the time frame will primarily depend on the Heart ascension principle. We could give you information on this alignment as part of the program to teach others, but even so it would not guarantee the Heart ascension. It would only be a guideline of its true pathing.

Maia: It would seem apparent from the above information that first, we must be very attuned to that still small voice within as to where we are being guided to locate, and secondly that the scenario about to unfold is perhaps even more dramatic than we had engendered in terms of the separation of the two worlds at LP-40.

We encourage all to truly understand the depths to which our compassion for others must reach as the events related to this transformation unfold, as there will be many Souls needing that compassion. Open your Hearts and ask to receive the "Gift of the Dove". Compassion for others is the perfect vehicle to raise your Heart consciousness. Learn what true compassion truly means. Do you feel a lightness and tingling sensation when giving to others, or does it feel like a painful experience at times? Understand that if there is heaviness in the giving then there is some area of your unconscious self (elemental magnetic) that is not in alignment with the Heart centered intent of the Higher Self. Practice the infinity breath meditation daily and know that with the infusion of Heart energy all else will be transformed.

Memory Seeding Activation & Retreat in The Valley of the Golden Disc
Crestone, Colorado July 19 to July 26, 1995

This will be a particularly powerful time to be here in the "Valley of the Golden Disc" as the ascension matrix of the planet has its main energies started on July 21. This date was chosen in accord with the startup of what is being referred to as the "Lazarus Manifold", or main ascension matrix of the planet by Tehuti/Thoth.

Tehuti and his Merkabah group "Chariot of the Sun" have announced the re- activation of first, the "Holy Doma" (see "The Seven Pyramids of Awakening" Temple Doors issue 3/4 -94), a seven pyramid complex comprised of pure gem stones which existed in Atlantis. One of these pyramids known as "Pashatasarak"ascended at the final demise Atlantis. It was the size of the Great Pyramid of Giza and constructed of pure kous Emerald. The re-activation of the "Holy Doma" will be accomplished by the Atlantean Ascended Masters known as "Orhamis" starting March 12, 1995 and will be completed July 15, 1995, setting the stage for startup of the "Lazarus Manifold" ascension matrix on July 21, 1995.

The Lazarus Manifold will be impacting humanity at the cellular level to restore our stellar orientation, or Universal diochromy. Our beings contain trapped starlight. Once this starlight is allowed to reorient towards "Home" we will become liberated entirely from our fallen light spectrum.

The Memory Seeding Activation will involve multiple dynamics. According to Tehuti there once existed a Sacred mountain range within what is now the San Luis Valley ("Valley of the Golden Disc"). This range was linked inter dimensionally to the "Golden Star of Mazuriel" (future consciousness that all the Pleiadians, Sirians, Orionians, Arcturians etc. hail from) At some distant time in the past this range was destroyed through an interdimensional cataclysmic event. The remains of the range eroded into what now comprises a sizable quantity of the sand in the Great Sand Dunes National Monument. These dunes are some of the largest on the North American continent. Each grain of this

"Sacred Sand" contains a hologram (memory seed) of the energy matrix of the entire mountain range that once existed.

On July 21, 1995 we will be working through an etheric pyramidal temple structure known as the "Templa Mar" which will be directly channeling the rays of pure "Solarian Consciousness" (the future third millennium or "Golden Age" consciousness). They will then resonate and be amplified through the sand crystals. We will be given specific procedures by Tehuti to resonate our DNA with these energetics effectively producing a phase lock to this consciousness and the planetary crystalline helix. We will be working with these energetics concurrent with the startup of the Lazarus Manifold as previously mentioned, which will help to "excite" the new stellar orientation on both a planetary and personal level. This will facilitate a very rapid progression into a new level of experience for those who participate directly. All energetics will be overseen by Tehuti and "Chariot of the Sun".

This activation/retreat with additional workshops, meditations and "Source Translated" information should provide for a well rounded week of personal/planetary transformational experience and a wonderful vacation in an exquisitely beautiful place. As part of our program we will be visiting and interacting with both Mt. Antero and the sacred Ute Indian structures.

The Spiral Tower
In the Baca Grande (adjacent to the town of Crestone, Colorado) is 80 acres containing a hill upon which arises a yellow-gold ziggurat (spiral tower) from the landscape, with the mystical Sangre de Christo mountain range, include majestic Mt. Blanca, in the background. The ziggurat was supposedly built by a young man from the Middle East who is the current owner of the property. He is said to have constructed it in memory of a lost love. Tehuti tells us that the geomancy of the Earth in this area, centering on the hill with the ziggurat, is especially powerful, and an anchor point to the center of the planet. One of the places we did temple work when I

first came to Crestone last year, was at the ziggurat.

Below Tehuti speaks on correlation between Glastonbury Tor in England and the ziggurat land in Crestone, Colorado, which he calls Auramur (literal translation: Heart Sun of the Mother Earth-Sea ... archetypal translation: Bridge of the Sun)

Tehuti: Glastonbury and Auramur are connected by a golden etheric cord of light called the Phakni. This was created by the Dannan eons ago in preparation for the future relocation of the Ark to the Valley of the Golden Disc. Glastonbury is the center of the Grail Mysteries on the Earth. Tor Hill is the center point of that center. In order for the Ark of Grace to complete its program of Light in the 2nd millennial World, it must be united with the codes contained in the Grail of Light.

The resonating disc of golden grid lines synchronizes and unites all Light engendered consciousness with the Sacred valley. It "reformats" this consciousness into a nesting or interlinking hologram which is separate from the base line of 2nd millennial reality. This process is gradually establishing a reality frame that will be an intermediary between the crumbling, Oritronic 2nd millennial and the future Metatronic 3rd millennial. The land we define here as Auramur contains the dynamic core link through Ziggurat Hill, to the sun atoma at the center of the Earth. This is the anchor or bridge of the sun that keeps the Golden Disc in balanced resonance with the center of the planet and its "Sun Rose" core.

Glastonbury, the font of the Crystal Isle of Avalon, contains some of the purest Light codes for the coming planetary ascension. These are embedded like fine, pearlized crystal beads in the sacred vestments of the land. In transferring these codes through the "golden cord" to Auramur, they must pass via Tor Hill, through the central sun atoma or "Sun Rose", upward through Ziggurat Hill to Auramur. This path of the Holy Fire transfigures the Light Codes of Glastonbury into a fiery shield of Diamond Light called the Huroiishavama. This is the merkabah of the Metatronic Lords of Light. Out picturing through Ziggurat Hill, the Huroiishavama is contained for the time being in a cell of brilliance which we shall call by its Mari name, Samtii, "the pearl house."

Interdimensionally, the pearl house is maintained beneath the ziggurat. It shields and protects the Huroiishavama, also masking the powerful Metatronic field projected from this merkabah, preventing it from disrupting the 2nd millennial reality still present in the San Luis Valley (Valley of the Golden Disc). At a future time this Diamond Light Shield will arise from its pearl house to create the merkabah field for the receipt of the Ark of Grace into its domain in the Sacred Valley.

Glastonbury is the main interface with Auramur through Ziggurat Hill, while other major sacred sites are accessed inter dimensionally. One of these sites is the "Crystal Tower" in the Valley of the Blue Star in Tibet, another the Magdalene Tower in Rennes Le Chateau, France.

Both Glastonbury Tor and Auramur's Ziggurate Hill are major entry points to the

Planetary Labyrinth Grid. This grid connects all labyrinths of pattern in the outer dimensions (as on the floor of Chartes Cathedral in France and the underground labyrinths that may be found beneath such sacred structures as St. Peter's Basilica in Rome) and the inner planes (such as the RA-UM, established by the Order of the Burning Bush through Tribelight: (see SOURCE issue 2-'88, predecessor to Temple Doors).

An excerpt from The Arthurian Tarot, A Hollowquest Handbook, by Caitlin and John Matthews:

Upon a high tor, a tower is struck by lightening, masonry falls to the Ground. But, while the physical tower is shattered, a spiral tower of crystal remains. About the tor, the signs of the zodiac glow within the land. An owl flies upward.

Surely "Ascension Lands" such as the Valley of the Golden Disc are poised between two worlds. As the planet as a whole moves toward Her destiny, those of us on the Sacred Lands must become Grail Knights who will move between these realms for the benefit of all. Glastonbury, England is the "Third Eye" or Brow Chakra Ascension Gate (see article on the Golden Taya, this issue) just as the major portion of the San Luis Valley, including Crestone and Baca Grande is the "Crown Gate". Thus we see a strong transference through the two Spiral Towers between the Vision and the ascension of that Vision into a new dimension of actualization.

The Oracle Tribe & the Living Light Ark
Tehuti has told me of an "Oracle Tribe" of Indians related to the Utes who once dwelt in what is now the Baca Grande/Crestone, Colorado region. These were a small band of Native Americans who erected stone chambers which still stand as energy portals to the past. Tehuti states that these small structures were not homes but resonating chambers occupied only for shamanic purposes by the Oracle Tribe. These people had been led into the region by a powerful shaman named Medicine Crow, who has appeared to me and at least one other (independent of the knowledge of Medicine Crow's presentation to me) individual I am

aware of in the area. There was also the "Grandfather" of the Tribe, a wizened Elder known as Bear Speaker. He has made himself known to me as well. Tehuti refers to these people as the Oracle Tribe, as every member was an oracle in some capacity. They were from several different but related origins, guided by an ultra being who brought them together in a singular purpose. This purpose was eventually to create a "Guardian Tribe" who would be Keepers of the Sacred Chamber within the Sangre de Cristo Mountains of the San Luis Valley. (Note: These "sacred chambers" are within the mountains, and do not refer to the stone resonating chambers built in the Baca by the Oracle Tribe.)

The Tuatha de Dannan who maintain these chambers were to leave this reality and return to the inter dimensional Avalonic realm. They needed to insure that the forces and knowledge within the Sangre de Cristo chambers would be maintained until their return to the Sacred Valley. By genetically mixing with the Oracle Tribe, the Dannan created the proper light genetics for the Guardian Tribe.

There will be those now reincarnated from both the Oracle and Guardian Tribes who will be returning to this region to continue evolving their role as guardians and emissaries for the "Path of the Ark of Grace" in its return to its thresholding chamber in the Valley of the Golden Disc. Some of these souls will feel guided to live in the Valley, others will come for specific interaction and then depart.

There are souls of these two interrelated Tribes who have chosen to remain disincarnate as "Spirit Holders" in the Sacred Valley. Interaction with these beings can lead individuals in finding their true work with the Ark. All humanity is linked through the archetypical light codes of the "Living Light Ark", which the Ark of Grace exemplifies. Each human being is an "ark" prototype of the Living Light Ark. Using the "TALMUD/TYCHON" meditation given in this issue will give you access into the Living Light grid of the Ark.

Revisiting the Talmud
And other information from Tehuti on some recent experiences

TEHUTI/THOTH: The land and ocean area risen or translated from this dimension (originally in Peru) in which is contained the first true Ark of the Covenant, we shall refer to here as the RISEN SEA. Within the Caverns of the Ark, there is suspended the TALMUD, a diamond-shaped blue quartz crystal. Near the TALMUD crystal is the TYCHON Flame, a large beam of high energy lasers streaming upward from a white stone lotus. The TYCHON is a balancer and rectifier of energies. It stabilizes the dimension in which the RISEN SEA abides and maintains a frequency of parity between the Ark and its parallel vector (this dimension). The TALMUD crystal is more complex to interpret. Its entire workings are not to be given at this time, but it operates in conjunction with the TYCHON. It absorbs Light into elemental conformity, all the while accelerating the quantum of Light transfer, which in turn, refines the entire process of Light to Spirit through its systems.

The TYCHON Flame ... is liquid Light, held back a moment before the rush of time. In it is contained the record of humanity's passing in the Earth. This knowledge is channeled through the crystal TALMUD as DIVINE LAW. It is segmented into verses of consciousness, each motion given a separate dialogue in time. The many souls incarnating again and again are the embellishment, the notes in a concert of spirit consuming flesh, singing in the flame of life that dwells but a moment with the reality of the soul.

The stage of soul evolution in Earth are divided within the crystal into four Sacred major parts, equivalent to the Four Forces of the Universe, the Four Elements of the alchemical Earth, and the Four Sons of Horus. I give you four words to speak, each a trigger to a fourth segment of the crystal. As you speak each word, take several minutes upon that word before proceeding to the next in order that you may place yourself into memory rhythm with that stage in your soul's evolution. Bring into your consciousness a visualization in tune with that experience.

Proceed through the four sacred force words applying this memory.

The words are:
ORIGIN ... TRIBULATION ...
TRANSFORMATION ... LIGHT

Thoth tells about the Golden Egg: This object was the size and shape of an ostrich egg ... the "egg" was of alchemical gold both inside and out, a layer of crystalline material pressed in-between these two layers. On the uneven edge of the "break" were tiny golden circuitry embedded within the crystal "filling". We were told by Thoth that this object was half of the entire unit. This half, with our help (and no doubt that enlistment of other sources as well) would be translated from the dimension of the RISEN SEA to this dimension. It would appear partly buried in a specific region of the Americas, to be found by a certain envoy or party unknown to us. The second half of the Golden Egg would be brought through at a future date and eventually united with the first half. When brought together the circuitry would be complete and the Ark of the

Covenant would be translated via this devise, into our dimension.

... the Guardians of the Sacred Grounds, high souls who once lived, and many who are still living (inner/outer Earth) as Great White Shamans (as opposed to "Black Art" Shamans) are gathering in the sacred places. They are awakening the magic of their ages in the Earth, following the Dreampath for Earth Awakening. They are closer at this time to our reality. All is stirring from the ancient vaults and minds of direction from long ago.

In 1989 the Ark of Grace (the True Ark) was translated into a chamber in Mt. Sinai, yet it remains undescended in its full unfoldment.

the "Medicine Wheel", a region of the United States with its center at the Four Corners. In ancient days these fragments had been charged by the Ark of Grace, and were to create an energetic field within the Valley of the Golden Disc (San Luis Valley of Colorado in the outer rim of the Medicine Wheel) for the coming of the Ark of Grace into a thresholding chamber within the Sangre de

Cristo mountains bordering the valley. At some point in time after the Ark is brought to its thresholding chamber it will be translated into this dimension.

Tehuti's 1995 update on the Ark of Grace, the Risen Sea, the TALMUD, the TYCHON Flame and the Golden Egg: The Risen Sea is the dimension that contains the chamber wherein the TALMUD and TYCHON are maintained. Originally in Peru, it ascended from your dimension in 12,500 B.C. This small region of only 3 1/2 miles across was the location of a group of Hyperborean Atlanteans known as the Atlanagas. They were related to the Rutan Atlanteans (Hyperborean), and contained more Sirian genetics with closer resemblance to the Lion-Ones (the family of Pashat, Zumir, Sun Lords, etc.). With their human –lionese features, they kept to their own remote area of South America, communing only infrequently with the Rutans. Their focus on the planet was to maintain the TALMUD and TYCHON, brought to this world from Sirius eons ago. The TALMUD and TYCHON held the calibration patterns for the Foundation Stars, those sun-stars in the universe which form the Zuvuya or return path of spirit to the center of the Universe. It is to this center that we must all return. The major Guardians of this quadrant of the Universe are Sirius, the Pleiades and Orion. All three of these stellar guardians have fallen zones within them, the guardianship remaining within the undescended regions.

In 12,500 B.C. (before the eruption in the Atlantean time grid, causing the Kali Time Rift) the 3 1/2 miles of the Atlanagas was translated into another dimension to protect the TALMUD and TYCHON from violation, as it was known by the Guardians that the tear in time would soon be outpictured through the Atlantean grid. Major configurations in the karmic balance of the planet took place in the year 12,500 B.C. which set the schematic in place for the ascension of what we call the Risen Sea.

Those who now have the first half of the Golden Egg are presently in New Mexico. They are called the Sariia, from the Pleiades. They are some of the star ones who walk amongst you. The second half of this computer devise is in Mt. Blanca (part of the Sangre de Cristos in the Valley of the Golden Disc). It will be revealed and brought together with its other segment in the future. You will be in communication telepathically with the Sariia, and working with them on a related project, soon.

The TALMUD, blue diamond crystal is actually not a full "quartz" mineral logically. It is a combination of both quartz and lithium and resonates at a frequency beyond both. The flashing double-diamond in place at the gateway of the vortex of the Golden Star Templa Mar (at Crestone/Baca in the Valley of the Golden Disc) is energetically aligned to the Talmud as a sacred geometry interface.

Maia: Briefly, how can humanity work with the TALMUD and TYCHON Flame for personal and planetary evolution?

TEHUTI: First, by visualizing the Blue Diamond Crystal and the TYCHON Flame, then focusing upon the words given: Origin, Tribulation, Transformation and Light, working with these procedures as given above. Once you feel resonant with this procedure and your body is experiencing an energy flow with your mind clearly aligned to the essence of the experience, you may begin the process of asking to be cleared of akashic forms (karmic) which are impeding your progress towards Divine Order. Allow the Blue Flame of the TYCHON, flowing through the "Mind" of the TALMUD, to cleanse all entanglements from your being. As you move through the Flame, experience the consciousness of the Earth blending with the blue TALMUD/TYCHON dynamic. Allow the sacred hum of the TYCHON to call forth the power from the center of the Earth (the central sun atoma). See it expanding upward in waves of brilliant Light to envelope the outer shell and atmosphere of the planet like an elixir of blue, green and gold. Call forth the Grandfolk Dolphins (high master beings in Dolphin form), linking them to form holographic patterns of morphogenic Light transfers through the crystalline grid of the Earth.

Maia: What is beyond the cellular, emotional and mental experience?

TEHUTI: The experience of the Attasic Universe.

Maia: Could you tell us more about the Attasic Universe/Light grid?

TEHUTI: The Attasic Universe is the Unified Field of all consciousness in which no separation dwells. The Attasic Light Grid is the organizational patterning for separate realities as they come together to create the Attasic dynamic.

Accelerating the Healing of Self Denial to a New Octave

On the evolutionary path of healing and denial or suppression of self, we are in essence acting out and releasing karmic tendencies or "samkharas" as they are known in the eastern traditions.

"SAMKHARAS: (aggregate of formations) a symbol associated with Dharma (karma). It usually signifies the transitory mental type-forms which change with every personality.

Impermanent truly are the Samkharas, liable to origination and decease; as they arose so they pass away; their disappearance is happiness."

The samkharas are built up over extended periods of incarnational experience repeating themselves in various different expressions. Each time the embodied soul acts out of these tendencies the magnetic patterning of that particular samkhara is strengthened. As our karmic incarnational experiences increased in number, so did the number and strength of the samkharas. Also, we had lifetimes where we were subjected to religious dogmatic austerities that demanded we suppress these building tendencies of the lower nature (self). Some of this teaching was well intentioned but resulted in the formation of energetic blockages due to the magnetic inner conflict. In other words, one aspect of our being was attempting to respond to its lower karmic nature while our conscious self with some level of Higher Self knowledge present, understood the need to transcend to higher levels of experience, but didn't understand the denying/suppressing that lower self component only added to the magnetic charge being held in the physical/emotional/mental bodies.

The emotional or feeling body is the primary consciousness interface between Spirit and matter. This statement is not complete, but for the purpose of this discussion I will utilize this model. The emotional body is intended to interface a spiritual reality into physical experience . It is a main connection between the "electric" frequencies of the Higher Self and the primal force magnetic energy of the manifest realms. The heart center is the gateway between realms, but the emotional body is the interface zone.

Anytime we have a had an experience in our incarnational experiences that we did not allow ourselves to feel completely, regardless of whether it was too painful, too joyful or anything in between, what has occurred is that we switch to the mental plane of experience to escape the feeling, and in essence stopped the flow of emotional "feeling" energy. When this occurs we have in effect froze the magnetic imprinting of that emotional energy in space and time. At some point that energy must be released to the Universal flow once again. This can happen in a number of different ways. Some of the more common methods of release involve bringing in a charge of energy that exceeds the amount of energy stored in the magnetic patterning and starting it in motion once again. This can be induced through any number of healing techniques, or by the Higher Self through painful experiences, if the conscious personality has worked (like "hello down there, if you can't hear me perhaps if we drag you through the briar patch.."). These magnetic patterns or "blocks" are actually an aspect of ourself that has now splintered off from our conscious awareness to have an unconscious (to us) reality all its' own. The existence of these unconscious magnetics is the primary reason that we seem to have events happening in our lives that we would rather not be experiencing, and many times do not understand. On the physical plane of manifestation the magnetic (feminine) component holds the true power to manifestation. If we are carrying around a plethora of magnetic patterns, unbeknownst to us they are drawing these events to us like two poles of a magnet attract each other. The divine gift in all of this is that when these events unfold we now have an insight into the unconscious aspect of ourselves that is not under the auspices of Higher Self so we can do something about it.

The self healing process has entailed getting in touch with our feelings and understanding what aspect of ourself is attempting to communicate to us through that feeling. Generally this aspect of self has not been recognized for some time, as it is a heavily conditioned pattern existing within the mass consciousness to ignore or suppress these feelings. The process of getting in touch with these feelings has been quite intensive for most of us, and in the intensity of the process there is the danger that yet another limiting pattern may set up in place of the one we have sought to transcend. This is an area whereby we must become creatures of thought and awareness, rather than creature of habit in order to go to the next octave of experience.

Let me expound on this a bit further. In the healing of self denials/suppression we have of necessity been appeasing some aspect of the lower self to satisfy the pent up desires that have been denied or suppressed over many lifetimes or experience. In this way we are able to act out the desires of the lower self and clear them. Herein lies an area that contains the possibility of becoming entrapped in a cyclical pattern that can recreate or strengthen the tendency (samkhara) or desire of the lower self. If we become enmeshed in this cycle it becomes difficult to see that much of the processing we are going through may be due to this process of cyclic recreation. Worse yet, we may actually have affected the satisfaction of these personal desire to such a degree that we become ensconced in the illusion of happiness that this has brought us to for the time being. This is where creating a solid intention to be aligned to the blueprint of ones Higher Self through regular meditation and affirmation upon this thought form is essential. With this intention fully registered upon the auric field, the process will unfold with less danger of the possible entrapments becoming actualized.

There comes a time when this process also must be accelerated to a new level. We must always be aware of the inner prompting emanating from the heart that indicates when it is time to adapt a new format within our process, lest we continue to emulate the past process for the sake of security to the process itself. Again, this involves moving beyond the realm of habit and into the expanded reality of thought and awareness in the "now"moment.

In relationship to the focus of this article, the next step happens when we are faced with moving to a new octave of experience in moving past the feelings of suppression of self. First, we must have developed the ability to feel and acknowledge these aspects of ourselves in the "moment" they are communicating to us. This means we must learn to be in the magical "now". When we have one of these feelings arise, it is imperative that we make it a priority in our lives to address it immediately, not tomorrow or at lunch time, etc. When we take this action of reprioritization we send a very strong message to Spirit that says, "Yes, I acknowledge that my most important job here is to fully integrate the Higher Self, all else is secondary to that mission." This can be reinforced with affirmations to that affect. When we put off dealing with our feelings to any other time frame but the "now", we send a contrary message to Spirit. When we have learned this agenda sufficiently, we are then ready to move into the arena where true magick is possible.

Within this next movement we come to recognize that identification of the aspect of lower self that we are feeling in the "now" holds a key to the transformation. By identification, I do not necessarily mean we must receive direct knowledge of the parameters of this aspect of self, but rather that we can locate it within our energy field/body through the feeling of it. In that moment, we are now faced with a decision. Are we going to appease this aspect of our lower self once again in order to prevent the occurrence of energetic blockages created through suppression or denial, or are we going to reorient this aspect of the lower self consciousness (elemental magnetics/samkhara) to the perspective of our Higher Self? This is the moment of magick, where all things are possible. The Higher Self perspective will see the situation as an opportunity to love and have compassion for self and others. From this perspective in the "moment" we experience the feeling of the lower self emerging, as it perceives it is being denied, we are able to bring the vibrations of the Higher Self into direct contact with this aspect of the lower self and transform it through the Law of Vibration. This law states that all higher vibrations will always transform the lower vibrations whenever they interact. In order for this to occur we must bring these vibrations together through our consciousness by "locking onto the feeling and at the same time accessing the greatest degree of Higher Self awareness possible in that moment. An affirmation such as "I now affirm I am ready willing and able to release this magnetic layer of consciousness currently being experienced to the complete transformation of my Higher Self", in addition to asking for assistance from the Angelics, Ultras and Masters who may be there to assist you can be very powerful in facilitating the process.

We must realize the incredible potential that exists in the "now"moment whenever these feelings are presented to us. This is the opportunity to walk through the doorway of eternal freedom, don't turn it away because something else seems more pressing or important, that is an illusion. Mass consciousness is heavily embedded with thought forms that tell us these feelings are a nuisance to be dealt with then we have time. This a product of the severely fractured karmic reality that we are living in. This consciousness is born directly of misaligned materialistic focus. This focus was born of survival needs as our ability to manifest from the ether slipped away. We have all participated in the descending order of events that have led us to this seemingly limited reality system. We must trust that in the reprioritization of our focus to make the matters of Spirit at least equally as important as third dimensional duties (with full integration as an objective), we will be fully supported from the higher aspects of our being in our needs to live physically upon this planet and go about our soul work. There are truly no obstacles to prioritizing our energy affairs in such a way as to be able to deal with feelings that arise in that moment, only excuses.

We must realize that this accelerated movement is a gateway to yet another realm of experience that takes us to the next level and so on ... infinitely. It is also time to breakdown and transform all thought forms that may subtly perceive "we have arrived at realization", as they only limit us, and the expectation engendered in these thought forms sets us up for disappointment at some future time. Realization will be a state of beingness non-reliant upon belief system thought forms.

Self discipline is an important component in the transformational process, but we must be aware of what it is we are disciplining ourselves to. Strictly adhering to any particular format has its benefits to be sure, but we must realize these are only tools to be used for a specific job and must be released when the time has come where they no longer serve us. The true discipline needed is not to any outer form, but to truly listen to the voice of the Divine within our own hearts, and allow that energy to permeate our experience. The heart energy is the most powerful transformational force in the Universe. By expanding this energy throughout our own beings, bathing them in the ecstatic embrace of Divine Light, we will successfully transform all lower vibrational magnetics and be able to achieve a truly amazing capacity for compassion in all our experiences.

Atlantean Crystals
As the ascended Emerald Pyramid of Ruta (the Pashatasarak) is light encoded back into the Holy Doma (Holy Dome of Light, see last Temple Doors issue3&4-94), all Atlantean crystals remaining on and in the planet which were originally programmed by the Doma are beginning to activate on a new level of consciousness. They are the "seed crystals" for alignment of the Earth/Human element to

the light grid of the 3rd millennium (future) time wave.

Many of these crystals are now in etheric retreats and the inner Earth, but some are still in circulation upon the surface of the planet. You may even possess one of these crystals without realizing it.

During the age of Atlantis, especially in its last years, most of these crystals were transported to other sacred areas of the planet to perpetuate the Earth's connection to the Attasic light grid or true light matrix of our spiritual creation. Although we have fallen from alignment with this grid, we maintain contact points through various sources left us by the ancients. Among these are the Atlantean Crystals and Dweller Crystal Skulls (see Temple Doors issues 4-90 and 1&2-92). Both will "open the scroll" to a new dimensional reality potential in their communication with the planet.

There are several main types of "Atlantean Crystals":

(1) Implanted crystals – These are crystals brought from Atlantis and physically implanted into the Earth at various locations, usually upon power nodes.

(2) Transference crystals – These are crystals still within the veins of the Earth. They have had the light codes of various sacred knowledge and other planetary continuum of the Atlantean programs encoded within crystal matrices in the Earth which are part of a vein Tehuti calls "Merlin's Mine". The crystals within Merlin's mine contain Light program encoding of various "stratum" for planetary transformation, one of which is Atlantean.

(3) Interfaced crystals – These are "ordinary" crystals which have been programmed to interface with the Atlantean stratum of the Merlin mine (or other stratum of this matrix).

Using any crystal that has been cleared of negative influence you may tap the Atlantean Crystal Matrix (ACM), which is a light net connecting all the Atlantean Crystals to the greater Attasic Universal Light Grid.

To aid you in accessing the ACM, visualize a blue-green light, in the center of which is a sparkling clear crystal radiating rainbow colors. Chant the mantram OMU- RA-SA-SET-TA until you feel you have successfully entered the matrix. Then chant AB-E-VEH-SEE-ME-KA-ON_UR-EH as you call upon these codes to quicken your light body to the Attasic Universe.

Preface

We will be relying primarily upon "source translated" material for the information base presented within this document. This information is complied from many years of work with the Soul-being we will be referring to as Tehuti. Master Architect of the Great Pyramid of Giza.

The concepts and energy structures that we will be presenting are of a multi- dimensional nature and are at best difficult to describe in linear terms, always presenting the distinct possibility of misinterpretation due to the confines of a three dimensional languaging system.

Due to this possibility we are first presenting some basic overall concepts that are important to understand as a premise to the greater body of information. Whenever possible we will refer back to these basic concepts to further clarify the overall perception that is needed. Those who have been following this information for a long time will already be familiar with some of these concepts.

The first concept that must be understood for the purposes of this work is that of the three millenniums. In higher dimensional reality systems time is experience in terms of events rather than linear years. We will be using the term "millennium" in a way that has a different meaning than that given in Websters Dictionary. A millennium will represent a series of events or energy movements, and can encompass many millions of years as in the first millennium, a few thousand as in the second millennium, or infinite potential as in the third millennium in terms of linear Earth time.

The first millennium is the period of linear time and all related events prior to the "fall" or decline in this creation zone from experience of the full Grace factor. This includes all realities that embrace this creation zone prior to the fall.

The second millennium was set in motion by the chain of events comprising the fall from Grace, culminating with the crucifixion of Christ, the true starting point of the second millennium. All of the second millennium is a karmic interim period sandwiched between the first and third millennium consciousness flows. It is somewhat of a detour that needed to be taken in order to reach the true destination.

The third millennium is the future reality that will begin at the point Tehuti calls LP-40*. This is recognized by many as the great transitionary moment when "the hundredth monkey effect" will take place. If you have not heard of "the hundredth monkey" effect, this is a projected point in time when the critical mass of awakened consciousness is reached that will catapult the Earth and all of its properly prepared inhabitants through a quantum leap into a higher dimensional experience, permanently. The third millennium is what has been referred to as "The Golden Age". Based upon information received recently from Tehuti, the third millennium will begin rather dramatically with considerably less overlap than experienced in the transition from the first to the second millenniums. According to Tehuti there will be an overlap of 15 days at that time. There is much more to be understood about the moment of transition into this reality system and the true nature of that future reality. We will be covering this in greater detail in the body of information to be presented in future issues.

The fall itself is a complex series of linked events that embrace realities beyond the planetary, and indeed even the solar (our sun) spectrum. In terms of Earth years the fall took place over many thousands of years, starting in early Lemuria and ending with the crucifixion of Christ. This scenario embraced the epochs of Lemuria and Atlantis completely. In terms of the ending of the first millennium and the beginning of the second millennium, there is no clearly defined point where this occurred, as there was an overlap in its linear time sequencing.

In truth, the first and third millenniums embrace the same Grace factor and consciousness vectors. The movement into the third millennium is akin to the closing of the circle, except that the circle is actually a spiral. As the cycle is brought to completion it is moved into yet another evolutionary cycle further up the spiral. It is our understanding that this is an infinite process within an ever expanding Universe.

Another concept that must be presented is that even though we are still measuring time in terms of years, the year of today is encompassing a greater segment of reality than the year of the past. All energy movement of this current linear time frame is greatly accelerated from that of even 100 years ago, not to mention many thousands or even millions of years back in linear time. This means that for any given linear time unit now, there will be a greater number of events (energy movements) that will have transpired than in the same unit in the past. Maia learned early on from the Ultra Terrestrials that when she was translating information from the holocrystallic recording crystals* of the Earth there was an adjustment that had to be made in the time sequences to account for this "time curve".

The ultimate truth is that all three of these periods of time are truly arranged in a spherical array of nodes on an infinite spectrum of reality, and as such are actually occurring simultaneously with one another.

The next concept needing explanation is that of Cosmic vs. Earth temple, and "temple" vs. "light net (grid)" vs. "function". You will see these terms appearing throughout this information as it unfolds and it is important to understand the difference to grasp the interactions between them.

A Cosmic temple format is described as a major organizing structure with its origins beyond the solar (our sun) spectrum of consciousness (ie. Archangelic, Seraphimic, Central Sun Solar Lord, etc.).

An Earth temple is described as a major organizing structure with it s origins within the solar (our sun) spectrum of consciousness, usually angelic. An Earth temple would differ from an Earth light net (grid) in that it reaches beyond the elemental (Devic) Earth grid into an overview perspective within its organizational scope.

A Cosmic temple differs from an Earth temple in that it organizes the Earth temple formats. Both are interactive directly with the Earth light grids, but in differing modalities. In other words, even though a Cosmic temple is organizing the Earth temple formats which in turn organize the Earth light grids, the Cosmic temple can still directly influence the elemental Earth light grids. This is a difficult multidimensional concept to grasp. Think of it as redundant computer systems aboard an aircraft. There is a linear sequencing that occurs in these systems during "normal" operations but any one of the components can run the whole show by itself if necessary. The

Universal flow can never be dependent upon linear sequences as the integrity of the whole is always considered.

A function differs from both temple structures and light grids in that the temple and light grids are like a number or series of numbers and the function is like the mathematical operandi (ie. Addition, subtraction, mulitiplication, division, etc.). In other words the temples and light grids hold certain codes and pathways and the functions are the energy/information that allows them to work and interact. Another analogy would be that the temples and light nets are like MacIntosh and DOS computer operating systems and the functions are the software that allows it all to be put into use and interface to be possible between systems. Again we have a situation of some overlap in linear terms as the temples have some "built in" software themselves. You might think of them as the base computer system you would buy that comes with the basic software package, but to realize the full potential of the system some additional software, and even peripherals are needed.

There is overlap in the organizational scope of these structures, and in the first/second millennium transition, it would be incorrect to say that these are clearly defined in a linear sense. We make these distinctions to attempt an interpretation of these subtle realities in our linear communication system.

The next concept deserving explanation is that of the Tetratryons*. In the outline of the hierarchical ordering of the temple/lightnet/sub-net that follows this preface you will see a symbol appearing in various locations similar to those appearing on the bottom of this page. This symbol represents the Tetratryon hyperspace inter-dimensional activity. We tried to represent this key factor to the best of our ability within the outline and drawings. Tetratryons are hyperspace tetrahedrons with open ends connecting to one another to form dimensional transference zones. The energy travels between different dimensions of reality through the Tetratryons. The Tetratryons are akin to the synapses in the hue-man brain transferring higher dimensional thought energy into a physical reality system experienced as thought/action. The Tetratryons are best described as a mini temple with its own built in functions. The main difference being that the Tetratryons do not organize other structures, nor is their basic structure organized by any of the formats covered within this information. They are however, arranged by the temple/light net formats in order to serve their purpose. You can think of this ordering as being similar to compression/decompression software that is arranged under the main program, allowing the flow of energy /information between the compressed reality system and the decompressed reality system, its constant presence invisible to the user. The Tetratryons do not "translate" information but conduct or transfer it from one dimension to another. The translation is done by sentient consciousness within that particular dimension. The Tetratryons will be elaborated on in more detail within the future unfoldment of this information in subsequent issues.

There will be a complete section included on the use of group synergy work, training and application. Synergy work is formatted so that groups of individuals can duplicate the temple grid dynamics allowing a harmonic link to be created between the microcosm of the group and the macrocosm of the temple/grid. These techniques allow the groups to become more effective interactive units with the temple/grids than would otherwise be possible.

We hope that this work will be of service to those groups and individuals who are specialized in their particular field and are searching for ways to "plug" their knowledge and expertise into the greater scenario for overall maximum effect.

The Metatronic Temple: All aspects of all temple/grid formats fall under the auspices of the Metatronic Temple. The Metatron is the overall template of spiritual concept and application. This temple format also contains components that serve as communication links throughout the entire system inclusive of its first, second and third millennium holoview*. This could be described as a picture in the "mind" of the temple as to the cohesion reference points of all three millenniums. The Metatronic Temple (or Metatronic Spiral*) conjoins with the Attasic Universe*, which is the unified field of consciousness where no separation exists. The Attasic light grid contains the organizational patterning to bring the separated realities back into their original state of unification.

The Metatronic Alpha Temple contains the light codes of the "full light" spectrum, whereas the other temple formats are working in various gradients of the "half light" spectrum referred to as the Oritronic Spiral* by Tehtuti. There is a necessary progressive linking of these various sub realities in order to effect the return of all systems to the full light Metatronic consciousness.

The Metatronic Temple has a main core beam which is a dynamic system of the Aaronrod (Arianrhod)* present within the greater Multiverse. Around the core beam is the

Metatronic Alpha-Omega Spiral*. "Alpha" because it is in a modality of specific function, and the "Omega" would be the completion of this specific function as it superlates* (total awareness being created as a separate field of experience from the formalizing body of events through the superheterodyning* process). It is the Alpha end of the spiral which interfaces most directly with the reality spectrum in this linear time frame. The core beam and Metatronic Alpha-Omega Spiral are positioned in alignment with the Celestial Meridian*. The smaller portion of the Alpha spiral is facing the south (micro) quadrant, and the larger portion of the Alpha spiral is facing the north (macro) quadrant.

By utilizing north and south as positioning descriptions we are not referring to the normal connotation of these terms, although there is a corollary. The Alpha end of the Alpha spiral is the large end and is aligned north to the star Theta Draconis in the constellation Draconis. The Omega end of the Alpha spiral is the small end and is aligned in the south to the star Epsilon Orinius, with Sirius as a calibration star. The Alpha end of the Omega spiral is the large end and is aligned to the Golden Star of Mazuriel*, existing in another dimension form ours at this time in linear reality. In a greater sense this is a repeating dynamic which winds its way through the Multiverse.

The Metatronic Alpha-Omega is a twin spiral with one phase (coil) referred to as the Atmic Red Serpent*(undulating current of the higher egoic, or Atmic, reality which superimposes upon our engramic* consciousness) and the other phase (coil) being the Shushumnic Blue Serpent* (undulating current of the infinity spectrum, which defines non egoic consciousness). In the Alpha end of the Alpha spiral the Atmic Red Serpent is the predominant spiral with the influence moving towards the Sushumic Blue Serpent gradually as you approach the Omega end of the Alpha spiral. This graduated shift continues throughout the Omega end of the Alpha-Omega spiral until full realization of the Shushumic Blue Serpent consciousness is reached.

If you visualize the Atmic Red Serpent at the Alpha/Alpha position being a very thick and luminescent line, and the Sushumic Blue Serpent as a very thin, almost nonexistent line, with the Red Serpent becoming thinner and less luminescent as it approaches the center "gate" between the two spirals and the Blue Serpent becoming thicker and more luminescent as it also approaches this "gate", you will have the concept. This dynamic continues on through the Omega spiral until at the Omega/Omega position the Sushumic Blue Serpent is the thick and very luminescent line while the Atmic Red Serpent is virtually nonexistent. Just beyond the Omega end of the spiral within the Golden Star of Mazuriel the Red Serpent has been completely absorbed into the greater reality.

The two phases of this spiral form an alternating current emanating from the core beam/Alpha-Omega spiral combination. In one phase the pulse is oriented to the higher egoic reality (Atmic Red Serpent) and in the next phase the pulse is oriented to the infinity spectrum (Sushumic Blue Serpent). In this way we are continually being programmed with the light codes of the full Metatron and those that "bridge" us to that reality of the future. It is important to understand that this pulsing of the alternating current actually involves a phase reversal whereby the two ends of the Metatronic Alpha- Omega spiral are switching positions (polarity) very rapidly. You might think of this as the 60 cycle alternating current in your home (USA). This alternating current is going through a phase reversal 60 times every second, but still maintains a positive and negative polarity within its overall orientation.

Note that there is an octahedron organized by each end of the Alpha-Omega spiral. For the purpose of this work we will be dealing primarily with the Alpha end of the spiral which contains the temple/grid formats.

The six points of the Octahedron organized by the Alpha spiral correlate to the six spatial time fields of the Arieopax*. The Arieopax and its relationship to these dynamics will be covered in more detail in subsequent issues.

The octahedron on the Alpha end of the spiral represents the current Earth reality, while the octahedron on the Omega end of the spiral represents the New Earth Star * reality that will exist after the LP-40 ascension of the planet. We will pass through the center "gate" of the two spirals at LP-40. All of our combined thoughts of love, harmony and peace are being recorded in this octahedron to form this new reality. Even those souls whom may not go through the gate at LP-40 are assisting in the creation of this reality every time they act or think out of love and compassion.

As covered in the article "The Golden Taya Allotments" (this issue), only twenty percent of the Earths land surface area contains the light coding necessary to move into the New Earth Star reality, with the remaining portion of the Earth going into an entropic decay pattern that will only last approximately 30 days in linear Earth time. The only portion of the energy matrix that passes through the gate into the Omega spiral octahedron is the Ascension Temple matrix outlined in the "Golden Taya" information. Not all the areas are listed of course. An area yet to be explored with Tehuti is the Rashel*/Bakhira* formats that correlate to the Ascension Temple.

It must be understood that the realization of the full Metatronic consciousness is quite some distance in our linear future. It is our current undertaking as a planetary consciousness to work primarily in the temple/grid formats falling under the auspices of the Alpha spiral that will link us to the full Metatron in time. We will therefore limit our discussion of the nature of the Metatronic Full Light Spiral to this brief overview in keeping with the intention of the International Magnetic Grid Ecological Emergency Network. For the reader who has interest in further knowledge of these dynamics we would refer you to "The Keys of Enoch" by J.J. Hurtak, Keys 107, 211, 318 and/or contact us directly.

Tehuti on the Rod of Noah

Maia: What exactly is the Rod of Noah?

Tehuti: This is a power geometric for installing "lightening paths*" into the planetary field.

Maia: How does the Rod of Noah apply in the Arkhom grid geometric?

Tehuti: Within this geometric no synergy groups are ready yet to access the Rod of Noah dynamic. It serves in the Arkhom as an anchor for the Metatronic Temple within the Oritronic fields.

Maia: Of what purpose are the lightening paths?

Tehuti: They can be employed to create everything from new dimensions and stars to reality sub-structures within existing dimensions. In the Arkhom, the Rod of Noah is merely a balancing template, however it has the capability via sentient consciousness working in synergy to create lightening paths at some time in the future in your linear reality when there are synergy groups able to handle this type of energy.

**2023 May - Dimensional experience -
Peter Roth explains my consciousness
level based on the Map of Consciousness**

Peter Roth has been doing a radio show /
podcast for decades and I had been invited to
do a few with him to date. One of the last ones
began before the actual recording started
when he held up a chart and explained to me
that he has been evaluating others after
having been evaluated himself. He told me
that I was a 725 that day and I didn't know
what that meant until I researched Dr David
Hawkins' book - Power vs. Force to
understand the Map of Consciousness.

Chapter 5 - Social Distribution of
Consciousness Levels **

General Description
A graphic representation of the distribution of
the respective energy levels among the
world's population would resemble the shape
of a pa-goda, in that 85 percent of the human
race calibrates below the critical level of 200,
while the overall average level of human
consciousness today is approximately 204.1

The power of the relatively few individuals near the top counterbalances the energy of the masses toward the bottom to achieve this overall average. Only 8.0 percent of the world's population operates at the consciousness level of the 400s, only 4.0 percent of the world's population calibrates at an energy field of 500 and over, and a level of consciousness calibrating at 600 and over is reached by only one in many millions.

At first glance, these figures may seem improb-able, but if we examine world conditions, we will quickly be reminded that the populations of whole subcontinents live at a bare subsistence level. Famine and disease are commonplace, frequently accompanied by political oppression and paucity of social resources. Many of such people live in a state of hopelessness calibrating at the level of Apathy, in resignation to their abject poverty. We must also realize that much of the remainder of the world's population— civilized as well as primitive-lives primarily in low vibrations.

** The level of consciousness of mankind as a whole remained at 190 for many centuries and then suddenly jumped to its present level of 204 after the Harmonic Convergence of the late 1980s. Did the rise in consciousness bring about the Harmonic Convergence? Did the Harmonic Convergence bring about the increase in the level? Or, did a powerful, unseen "implicate order" attractor field bring about both phenomena?

Any increased infusion of the influence of truth into the collective human consciousness gives us cause for greater hope than may be apparent from what tends inevitably to be a rather gloomy over-view.

We have established that consciousness is capable of discerning any change of energy to a degree of log 10 (to the minus infinity). This means that there is no possible event in the entire universe that is not detectable by the exquisite sensitivity of consciousness itself. The energy of human thought, though minute, is nonetheless absolutely measurable. A thought that emanates from the consciousness level 100 will typically measure between log 10-800 million to 10-700 million microwatts. On the other hand, a loving thought at the consciousness level of 500 measures approximately log 10-35 million microwatts.

Although only 15 percent of the world's population is above the critical consciousness level of 200, the collective power of that 15 percent has the weight to counterbalance the negativity of the remaining 85 percent of the world's population. Because the scale of power advances logarithmically, a single Avatar at a consciousness level of 1,000 can and does, in fact, totally counterbalance the collective negativity of all of mankind.

Kinesiologic testing has shown that:

One individual at level 700 counterbalances 70 million individuals below level 200
One individual at level 600 counterbalances 10 million individuals below level 200
One individual at level 500 counterbalances 750,000 individuals below level 200
One individual at level 400 counterbalances 400,000 individuals below level 200

One individual at level 300 counterbalances 90,000 individuals below level 200

12 individuals at level 700 equals one Avatar at 1,000

At the original writing of this book, there were twelve persons on the planet who calibrated over 600. In May, 2006, however, there were only six: three between 600-700, one between 700-800, one between 800-900, and one between 900-1,000.

Were it not for these counterbalances, mankind would self-de-struct out of the sheer mass of its unopposed negativity. However, the difference in power between a loving thought (10-35 million microwatts) and a fearful thought (10-750 million microwatts) is so enormous as to be beyond the capacity of the human imagination to even comprehend. We can see from the analysis above that even a few loving thoughts during the course of the day more than counterbalance all of our negative thoughts by their sheer power.

From a social-behavioral viewpoint, as we said, truth is a set of principles by which people live, regardless of what they might say they believe. We have seen that there is subjective truth, operational truth, hypothetical truth, and intellectual truth; and then there is factual truth. The legitimacy of any of these is dependent on the context of a given perceptual level.

Neural Network: The interlocking patterns of interacting neurons within the nervous system.

Neurotransmitters: Brain chemicals (hormones, etc.) that regulate neuronal transmission throughout the nervous system. Very slight chemical changes can result in major subjective and objective alterations in emotion, thought, or behavior. This is the prime area of current research in psychiatry.

Non-duality: Historically, all observers who have reached a consciousness level over 600 have described the reality now suggested by advanced scientific theory. When the limitation of a fixed locus of perception is transcended, there is no longer an illusion of separation, nor of space and time as we know them. All things exist simultaneously in the unmanifest, enfolded, implicit universe, expressing itself as the mani-fest, unfolded, explicit perception of form. These forms in reality have no intrinsic, independent existence but are the product of perception (that is, man is merely experiencing the content of his own mind). On the level of non-duality, there is observing but no observer, as subject and object are one. You-and-I becomes the One Self experiencing all as divine. At level 700, it can only be said that "All Is;" the state is one of Being-ness; all is consciousness, which is infinite, which is God and which has no parts or a beginning or end.

The physical body is a manifestation of the One Self which, in experiencing this dimension, had temporarily forgotten its reality, thus permitting the illusion of a three-dimensional world. The body is merely a means of communication; to identify one's self with the body as "I" is the fate of the unenlightened, who then erroneously deduce

that they are mortal and subject to death.
Death itself is an illusion.

2023 May - Dimensional experience - time dilation during Faery Falls hike in Mt Shasta

https://40kftview.com/faery-falls-hike-near-mount-shasta-dimensional-noise-230514/

The Hike – Sunday May 14, 2023 – Faery Falls near Mount Shasta

It's been a few weeks now since my last visit to the Mt Shasta area and there was going to be some evidence I'd be able to share with others of the presence of dimensional energies. This instance, like others I've had before will be in the Mt Shasta area. I'm particularly fond of waterfalls and so the opportunity to hike to Faery Falls presented itself. But everything happens for a reason … I'm about to show you what David Wallace explained to me as a "time dilation". I felt I was definitely in an energetic vortex … who knew I'd capture it on video.

Waterfall conditions in the area (McCloud, Hedge Creek and Faery Falls) were all spectacular – I've been here several times but never experienced that amount of water or energy. Finding elevated vibrations (energetic vortexes) in the Mount Shasta area has always been apparent for me from my first visit. Now it is becoming more frequent and as promised – greater contact from higher beings within Inner Earth and surface beings capable of matching that vibration will continue.

More evidence of these conditions will be provided for your own discernment as it is becoming available.

Along the line of things I experience but cant't explain in terms easily digestible for others ... there were strong elemental higher dimensional energies present I've sensed before. I have images of sprites in the forest over the course of my visits that some of you have seen. The aura along the trail leading up to the falls just seemed "Lighter".

My intention was to record the entire hike from the parking area all the way to the falls. For those of you that have been there before, you'll have an opportunity to see the falls in full-out flow – and for those who have never seen it, here's how you get to the falls on video. In my experience, I thought the hike would take about 25 minutes. I broke the hike into multiple shorter clips, I knew I'd be stopping often to gather myself as the hike is all about elevation gain, so they would provide the perfect place to stop and then begin recording again. In the end, there were 19 files varying in length from under one minute to the longest being 8:08. According to the time stamp on each video file I had taken, all totaled was 30:56. Made sense at the time – until I went to stitch the files together.

Now it's important to know that I sensed some dimensionally elevated energy on the trail, but I've found that a lot in different areas of Shasta. When I took all those clips and put them end to end as one movie, it's over 171 minutes long – I did not film it in SloMo ☐but that's how each clip behaves after initially starting at normal speed each one slows to a crawl in 3D time ... I was using default video settings on my iPhone 13 Pro Max with a gimbal I was practicing with. Dave Wallace suggests it's captured video evidence of a time dilation. Let that sink in. It was similar to traveling to Telos in Inner Earth in terms of linear time.

When I began to share the experience with a few Tribe I trusted to get some perspective, more than one referred to the scenes at the end of the movie Contact when Dr Arroway was testifying to her experience. There were synchronicities. It's not like extraordinary experiences haven't been documented around me before. This was the first time it was in video form.

Contact analogy

Hearing room scene:

Ellie: "I had an experience ... I can't prove it ... I can't even explain it ... but everything that I know as a human being ... everything that I am tells me that it was real ... I was given something wonderful, something that changed me forever ... a vision of the Universe that tells us undeniably how tiny and insignificant and how rare and precious we all are ... a vision that tells us that we belong to something that is greater than ourselves ...

that we are not – that none of us are alone … I wish I could share that … I wish that everyone if even for one moment could feel awe and humility and hope … but – that continues to be my wish. "

Committee member: "I assume you read the confidential findings report from the investigating committee … I was especially interested in the section on Arroway's video unit … the one that recorded the static … that fact the it recorded static isn't what interests me … what interests me is that it recorded approximately 18 hours of it … "

Final iMovie project is 171 min 21 sec
19 files – last four unaffected by the phenomenon in the first 15

[From Dave Wallace
The following link "appeared" on my phone immediately after linking up with KYMJYM telepathically. I asked him about soft metal coverings for a ship …

News flash from Taurus science council.

David ... time is a particle that is in permanent emanating sequence located within the zeroth point of the known universe.

Time has structures yet no perceived shape.

Tell your friend he was bathed in what we know as Anti-Chronotons.

Anti- Chronotons are used by B.E.S. (Beyond Earth Sentients) to observe your species and eliminate observation within a controlled radius of the specimens to be observed ...

Well, Lowell, that's it.

That's what it's like for me when I receive a message.]

Playback during dilations are Immersive – pay attention to nature reflecting sound codes. If you wanted some evidence of dimensional experiences – well here you go. No one was more surprised than me when I captured what I did and this time in a video format. More of these instances will continue in these areas for those vibrating at that level.

The following is an analysis of the video –
where each clip began, where each dilation
began and when normalcy was restored. It's
the Capricorn in me to understand fully this
particular rabbit hole so that I can explain it
for others.

0:00:00 recording commences
0:00:18 time dilation 18 sec in
0:11:19 restored
0:11:37 next clip commences
0:11:48 time dilation 11 sec in
0:19:22 restored
0:19:35 next clip commences
0:20:47 time dilation 12 sec in
1:06:17 restored
1:07:31 next clip commences
1:07:43 time dilation 12 sec in
1:15:38 restored
1:15:51 next clip commences
1:16:27 time dilation 36 sec in
1:39:55 restored
1:40:33 next clip commences
1:41:12 time dilation 39 sec in
2:06:27 restored
2:07:08 next clip commences

2:07:11 time dilation 3 sec in
2:08:11 restored
2:08:13 next clip commences
2:08:17 time dilation 4 sec in
2:10:19 restored
2:10:23 next clip commences
2:10:54 time dilation 31 sec in
2:30:35 restored
2:31:06 next clip commences
2:31:13 time dilation 7 sec in
2:35:54 restored
2:36:02 next clip commences
2:36:05 time dilation 3 sec in
2:38:08 restored
2:38:12 next clip commences
2:38:22 time dilation 10 sec in
2:45:06 restored
2:45:16 next clip commences
2:45:20 time dilation 4 sec in
2:47:30 restored
2:47:30 next clip commences
2:47:35 time dilation 5 sec in
2:49:16 restored

2023 Jul - Dimensional experience - Sharula Dux presentation

https://40kftview.com/the-making-of-sharula-dux-lemurian-princess-on-atlantis-lemuria-inner-earth-and-telos/

https://youtu.be/JmEjgfl9Ld4?si=W_rJArvnJ_BcQexz

Here is where my journey intersected with other Lemurians from Telos living on the surface:

For those of you just catching up to the existence of Inner Earth, Lemurians, Telos and the like ... what follows is the last known audio recording of a Lemurian originally from Telos living among the surface. In all my research, Sharula seemed to be the last person claiming to be such who came into the public awareness from the early 90's until she dropped off the radar again somewhere between 2005-2007. Knowing what I now know I am certain she retuned to Telos to wait out the final unfolding of the Shift from a higher vibrational environment.

Stay tuned ... had I mentioned before that the Lemurians said they intended to make greater contact with those on the surface capable of holding a high enough vibration to as to experience everything in that realm? Here it where it seems to be beginning to manifest.

In my research, Sharula was the last person I could find evidence of – that had had contact on the surface ... until last week. ☐

Maria (antaj'lilnair), daughter of Adama, shows up to visit Dianne Robbins

I have been looking for evidence of other Lemurians like everyone. Rob Potter had asked me back in October of 2020 if I knew of Sharula Dux. I kinda half-heartedly listened to her original presentation on a YouTube channel that posted it 15 years ago. It was chopped up into 12 – ten minute audio tracks from her 1993 tape. At the time, it appeared to be a rabbit hole not worth pursuing as my due diligence on her stopped somewhere either in 2005 or 2007 when she again dropped off the radar.

Reset the wayback machine to last week when I was having some text message exchanges with Dianne Robbins where she was telling me about Maria who came to physically see her that week. Dianne indicated that she had shared my contact information with Maria and in return gave me Maria's number.

An hour or so later after I had some time to assimilate this news, I reached out to Dianne asking her if I could reach out to Maria. Before I got a text response from Dianne, I received a text message from a previously unknown number saying it was Maria – Dianne's friend. Maria among other things is another Lemurian currently on the surface, she is Adama's daughter and happens to be Sharula's sister. The part of our exchange that struck an energetic chord was when she shared "my telosian name was antaj'lilnair"

Now perhaps you can begin to understand my haste and obsession to know everything I can about Sharula in preparation before moving on to the next physical connection to Lemurians on the surface coming my way.

This is what flowed through me to share with everyone ...

2023 Jul - Dimensional experience - 9 Inner Earth cities video shorts
https://youtube.com/playlist?list=PLLprvWl SpLImvLKlCAapCGWVjY1EzD9uE&si=U9q1A UIAEtWaYbYx

2023 Jul - Dimensional experience - witnessed a wormhole in the sky with craft passing through it during CE5 / Orb interactions at Jami & Corey's, McCloud, CA

2023 Aug 9 - Dimensional experience - opened a multidimensional time lock for souls fleeing the Western Canada fires

2023 Sep - Dimensional experience - awareness of my Soul timeline during Earth incarnations

Starbuck's Soul Journey for Gaia and Humanity

Through a series of past life regressions and multidimensional experiences since 2020, I have reestablished my 'original human blueprint' DNA access to those dormant parts of my Akashic experiences and here is how I see them coincide with Earth's evolution.

It explains clearly where and how humanity finds itself here through the timeline of Earth's development. This is what was revealed through the roles I've played in Gaia's evolution. It certainly answers why I am here and what space I am holding:

For purposes of understanding the following narrative, I will assume you have a command of the ideas of reincarnation and therefore the reality of past lives ... it's from that framework that I jump right in ...

I originated as a (now) future version of my soul (starseed) from the Pleiades, specifically the planet Taygeta, with connections to the Blue Star 'Rigel' in the Orion constellation and also the star Antares. Over lifetimes I evolved to the level of Melchizedek High Priest. The Melchizedek Order is the Universal connection to Source governed by the Law of One and Keepers of the Light. The vibratory level of the Pleiades is that of Melchizedek teachings – those being a clear connection to the cosmic principles of the Law of One and a comprehensive understanding of the Alchemy of Light with its influence on all Universal sentient life. My Pleiadian me evolved from Initiate to Master from within Thoth's original Mystery School – the Craft of the Brazen Serpent.

Earth has always been part of the Intergalactic Federation (largely 7D beings primarily – holographic beings and craft). Original Earth (which was/is Inner Earth aka Agartha) was a satellite station for the intergalactic fleet. It was already in a Seventh Dimensional state where masculine and feminine energies were perfectly balanced.

Nearby motherships were like arks. Earth was to be an experiment to see how human life would evolve here, and first visitors had to agree to a contract to participate in an experiment of life on earth.

When the Cosmic decision to develop Earth as a life-supporting planet (it wasn't the original choice for within our solar system) came along, I was presented with the opportunity to assist in the build-out of the Earth's mantle as I was embodied with advanced levels of biological science, alchemy and physics. The Pleiadians were known in this part of the Universe as Master Botanists and they were to be the go-to group to turn to.

The Dweller (you've heard reference to Him/Her in the Emerald Tablets) was given Universal authority for Earth's manifestation into life sustaining form. He/She selected the Pleiadians to initiate this function. The entity soon to become Earth had previously served as an interstellar satellite where galactic travelers would stop within this solar system on their way to other corners of the Universe.

The Dweller was a 9th Dimensional High Priest who had been initiated into the Melchizedek Order and ascended through the evolutionary stages to Mastery level when he/she was chosen by the Galactic Federation to oversee the Earth experiment. The evolution of a race of humans was to be one of the primary projects, to observe how they would evolve within this environment. The rest of the Universe will be watching ... Understand that Earth herself is an evolving sentient being and She was about to be initiated into the Melchizedek order and evolve as well. She bound herself (like all of us) to the Truth of the Law of One and the existence of the Light.

When I excitedly agreed to be a part of earth's development, it was because it would be designed metaphysically just like the stars in the Pleiadian system along the Order of Melchizedek. Every soul is truly a service-to-others spark connected to Source Light energy. The planets within the Pleiades were multidimensional beings based on the Universal Law of One and Masters of the Light. Each new planet would start at the lower density with lower consciousness to begin (obviously) as opposed to the more advanced planets whose dimensional ranges reach into double digits. Earth would begin with dimensional representations from the 1st through the 9th (we are currently moving from 3rd through to the upper octaves of the 4th). That's why we say humanity is heading into the 5th dimension because you're so close to equaling that consciousness vibration level. Once the mantle was formed and capable of supporting life – it WAS Eden as we imagined it to be. This initial civilization on Earth would be known as Elysium. As one of the botanists responsible for the outcome of this magnificently beautiful planet, I wanted to stay to enjoy the environment I had a hand in creating. So I petitioned the Galactic Federation along with many other scientists and their families to colonize on the planet.

Our request was to be granted with the understanding that Earth was an experiment for humanity to see how they would do given an environment of Sovereignty and Freewill. And so the first colonists would be Pleiadian to also serve as guardians of the Melchizedek

Light influence on Earth. Hence my eternal dedication to Gaia first. Soon the Pleiadians would be followed by the Lyrans. Now if you know what was going on cosmically at the time, the Lyrans had experienced planetary catastrophes too that made their planet no longer habitable. They first made their way to Sirius and were welcomed there to continue their evolution. When news about the new environment on Earth got out ... they were among those who petitioned to colonize after the Pleiadians were granted permission. There was interest in the Lyran influence after the original mantle build-out as the Lyrans were known to be Master Architects and Master Builders. (Do you see the cosmic synchronicities at work here?). When the Pleiadians with their knowledge of sacred geometry and electromagnetic cosmic energy worked along side the Lyrans to map out a grid on the planet to nourish it – they would be the builders of the energy centers leveraging the celestial positions – capable of direct connections to other locations in the Universe. The Pleiadians designed it and the Lyrans built it. This grid was designed to vibrate fundamentally at a 7th dimensional level as the Sun Disk placed in Earth to serve as its atoma came from the Seventh Galaxy of the Seventh Central Sun (the Sun of Illumination) and holds all Universal knowledge. Earth would be its future cosmic record (Akashic) keeper in the Halls of Amenti thanks to arrangements made by Thoth.

ELYSIUM
Elysium – first civilization on Earth and literally paradise on earth. Adhered to the Law of One within a beautiful loving environment where we didn't think to harm each other or anyone else. One's Sovereignty was assumed and honored.

Wars of heaven broke out by those who believed they were greater than Source and did not want to adhere to the Divine – we now call them the Dark Ones.

Destructive – Elysium had to be evacuated ... earth was thrown out of orbit due to a planet between Jupiter and Mars blowing itself up, causing ripples of chaos within the Universe ... only the Inner Earth survived intact – so you see the planet has fallen victim to cosmic physical disturbances that were unanticipated previously.

The Lyrans whose own planet was blown up and uninhabitable – fled to Sirius and then from Sirius received permission from the Galactic Federation to come and settle on earth. Built on what was left of Elysium, they were megalithic builders – the Lion people (very tall / some over 20 ft tall) with reddish hair and coppery skin, Master architects and builders of the hanging gardens, pyramids and the pyramid energy grids.

AVALON
Avalon (the next 7th dimensional civilization to follow Elysium – centered near Spain, Portugal, France territories) rose into a peaceful matriarchal society. Wizards (such as Merlin and Melinda), the Druid high priests and priestesses (benevolent elemental shape shifters) and the Mer (mermaid and mermen) formed there under the Law of One. The planet vibrated at a level of the perfect balance of Feminine and Masculine energies and it was sacred knowledge that the

Feminine Divine was the direct connection to Spirit and it was the honor of Divine Masculine to carry out the Divine message as received through the Feminine.

LEMURIA
Lemuria rose with this sentiment in the area we associate today as the Pacific while Avalon was in its prime.

Lemurians were highly sophisticated and androgynous (male and female within one body that was perfectly balanced). They were a 12'-14' ft tall being (in our 3D way of comprehending measurement), 7D, loving, gentle race of crystalline Light beings. Connected intuitively to the vibration of the cosmic grid. Built crystalline cities – worked with mother earth in a harmonious stasis – they lived Universal Oneness – never destroyed any forests, they incorporated into the environment – living with Prana (life breath) and achieving immortality more than a thousand years old.
Avalon – the peaceful place that never had to defend itself, was invaded by a race from Mars, who focused on the feminine

priestesses because they were familiar with the power of elemental energies. Atlantic Ocean appeared because of the destruction of Avalon and the islands of Atlantis began to rise under the influence of dark maji.

ATLANTIS
Atlantis could no longer reach that 7th dimensional state of being (that was in a frequency band that was inaccessible to them at their 5th dimensional vibration). Yet this was the vibrational nature of Earth during the most recent past Golden Age of Atlantis. Now there were male and female beings but balance needed to be restored – so that brother won't fight against brother anymore (remember the Lion kingdom) and when you reach the state where you don't need to fight anymore you can actually ascend into the 7th again.

Our dear Atlantis in the end was responsible for us all paying the price for following the non-Light. Hopefully history will finally reflect the lessons Atlantis should have taught humanity. To finally master the lessons of the Lion kingdom (duality) and Elysium (connection to All) after learning the lessons involving the wars of heaven – not to repeat those lessons again but to reach that state of Oneness to activate ascension back into the 7th dimensional realm in order to merge with Lemuria again.

So you had the Golden Age of Atlantis where everything was peaceful, beautiful and everyone worked in harmony and did not harm Mother Earth – when they built their crystal pyramid temples with their 5D high technology (which is now reawakening) and they worked as one.

You had the islands of Atlantis – many of those were the peaks left of Avalon and a lot of them still had the ancient teachings of Avalon and the Lion kingdom and Lemuria, but at the 5th dimensional state they couldn't quite understand it anymore.

The same beings that started the wars in heaven and the destruction of Avalon – they started to infiltrate the minds of humanity again (like a virus), when they get into your brain they start to control your ego and once they control your brain they begin divorcing your mind from your heart – that's exactly what happened in Atlantis and why humanity has been stuck here for sooo long.

I wanted to address the topic of the Nagas – the Serpent People, as humanity owes them a great debt of gratitude and appreciation for the wisdom they gave us. That is why you see its influence in early Egypt – those Egyptian deities honored where their wisdom came from. I hold connection to the Nagas and much gratitude for their role in humanity's evolution. They were what some characterized as the Serpent People from a planet called Sarpa Loka. They stayed and shared their vast Akashic wisdom with humanity through its early stages until the introduction of the dark energies taking souls in a non-Light direction. They left ... but their legacy of intuitive influence and wisdom remains. I carry Blue Cobra energy that some of you do too, if your kundalini has risen you know the sensation. They have not ruled out returning once we achieve the next vibrational level.

ADAM AND EVE

The story of Adam and Eve and the Tree of Life tells you about Atlantis – the Serpent always belonged to the Divine Mother (Sophia) and was always the sign of highly evolved knowing and knowledge which the Divine Feminine held, you see the serpent is everywhere on sacred sites – as is the spiral because that is spiraling energy that the Divine Mother holds which is the energy that holds the electromagnetic currents (the Telluric currents) which is the energy that was used in their spacecraft and every dwelling – it was actually tapping into the power that held Creation together.

When they say that the serpent actually came and asked Adam whatever and then Eve, the truth was – that it was Adam who got himself involved with those Ones who were mind controlling him and there, the seeds of dissent were sown into Adam's mind, (his ego began introducing thoughts of: 'do I really need to adhere to the Law of One? am I not greater than my Creator? I am more than the Father that created me, I can do better than he can') You'll come to know this faction referred to as the Belial ... that's a competition of the

masculine ego that comes into form and being
– actually Eve had nothing to do with it – it
was Adam that was being seeded the thoughts
of dissent, which he swallowed – in other
words, he became the dissent. He started to
actually divorce himself from the Divine and
he divorced himself from the female.

But what Jewish mythology tells us is that he
was first married to Lilith, because Lilith was
his partner he was first given by the Divine.
Lilith was a very strong and able woman – she
absolutely embodied the Divine Feminine
because she always held 'you are not more
than me ... we are equals' and she refused to
bow down to his wishes if she saw it was not
within Divine Will. She stood up and said you
are going the wrong way – so what did Adam
do? He complained about her in the highest
degree and said 'you gave me the wrong wife'
(see how he was already dissenting against
the Divine?) He was questioning the Divine in
all and everything – that is how you start
separating your inner knowing from your ego
that is questioning everything. It's not bad to
question but you've also got to listen to your
intuitive voice or inside – he was ignoring

that intuitive side and said 'I want to have another wife' – so he was given Eve, more pliant and more submissive but then he didn't like Eve either because he eventually accused her of bringing him into sin – which she never did. It was he himself who had this inner turmoil where he could not govern himself – that is where basically patriarchy starts.

That's exactly what happened during this period in Atlantis, patriarchy started taking over. Those entities started persecuting the High Priestesses and the feminine influence. The Melchizedek Priesthood stood together behind the scenes and said we will not allow this because they saw what was happening.

Thoth is there. When the Priests had the fore vision with what would happen to Atlantis (they saw they would destroy themselves and take most of humankind with them because of the mind control by these black maji who originally sowed the seeds of duality in Atlantis). The High Priests among the Light who had the gift of prophecy could see what a great calamity this would result in. Humankind is not mastering that lesson.

Instead of going up into the 7th they are going to descend into darkness, fall into 3D duality. The Priests knew they had to keep the seeds of enlightenment (illumination) alive – so they dispersed all over the world and they started planting colonies all over the world in places they knew they would be able to survive the floods that they knew would come.

Black maji (dark energies) were planting control boxes in the cranium area of the neck where they actually divorced your higher chakras from your lower chakras so you couldn't access your heart anymore. You were totally in the mind and controlled with external influence.

In a sense the populous allowed that to happen because you are a Sovereign human in this experiment with free will, but still tried to stay true to the Law of One.

EGYPT
Ancient Egypt was very important because Thoth was directed to go there next and salvage ancient technologies not only

Atlantean, but Akashic records and technologies of Lemuria and many other earlier civilizations on Gaia. They will eventually be kept beneath the Great Pyramid in the Halls of Amenti which we know from the Emerald Tablets. Thoth was instructed to use 'arks' that were like spaceships that could burrow underground. They created underground tunnels and cities that are still there all throughout the planet.

Preparations were continuing to be made as they knew that when the floods came they had to go underground in some places – like they had in the Himalayas (Tibet), Euro Mts in Russia, Incas, Mount Shasta.

Not all Atlanteans are dark – that's important to remember about our connection to Soul Tribe there. In fact the positive effect Atlanteans will help to restore with surface dwellers in 5D will be just as important as what the Lemurians in Telos promise to share with us. But the worst part of Atlantis' lessons are that those actions destroyed Lemuria as well and they can't be ignored. – It was the black maji who found their way into naive

Atlantean awareness ... and they were the ones that sowed seeds of dissent into the Lemurians. The Lemurians had everything they wanted and could manifest anything into form and being they liked – they did not have two separate bodies, the male and female form.

The black maji actually came up with the idea that the Lemurians connection to Spirit couldn't be all that perfect if they didn't experience physical sensations i.e. the sensual nature between male and female. Remember the Lemurians were 7th dimensional androgynous beings with a balance of Divine Feminine and masculine energies. The maji believed if they could convince the Lemurians they lost out on the experiences of sexual energy to mate that they could alter them so they could experience that physicality. Of course they would have to drop to at least 5th dimensional form in order for them to have those experiences and therein was the error the maji made when they cut themselves off from 7th dimensional frequencies they could no longer reach. They implied to the Lemurians that the Divine didn't make them perfect, which was a total lie – but they were about to forget they were more perfect than the Atlanteans in their androgynous form.

Regrettably, through their naivety the Lemurians fell for splitting themselves into two forms with help from the Atlanteans to experience physicality.

The tragedy of the Lemurians is that they fell for the black maji Atlantean's idea of separation as once they were separated they could never get back to that Divine Soul level again from within the 3rd dimension. They would try desperately to reach this spiritual level through relationships with other partners and in that, pain and suffering were created which they never ever knew before.

With that the Atlanteans began to enslave the Lemurians because the Atlanteans wanted their technology – the door was already closed to that within higher dimensional realms but they were trying to get it by force and to use it in self destructive ways.

Crystal Technology – in Atlantis they abused crystals and used them in atomic lasers that blew portions of the planet – the Divine Mother told the High Priestesses of Atlantis and those of Lemuria that stayed true to bury these crystals in the earth and seal them off so that nobody can access them until the time when humanity returns to the purity of love, unity and harmony and has the consciousness again to create paradise on earth and not destruction. Then these materials will once again surface. Look for them in Andara and Lemurian crystal form.

So those crystals were literally sealed off and so many of the souls that are incarnated now were the ones that sealed them off but the challenge now arises again – are you still going to be in duality or will you be in that unity consciousness field?

LEMURIA
Many higher dimensional beings would visit earth and some would leave lasting impressions both good and bad. It was to have its effect on humanity's evolution and to say it stunted humanity's growth would be an

understatement of vast proportions. The next civilization to assemble on my timeline is Lemurian from Mu. I am certainly glossing over Mu – Lemuria, as a comprehension of our soul paths through those civilizations deserves more than a footnote. The contributions to humanity made by Lemuria are immeasurable. Lemurians were 12'-14' ft tall (by 3D standards of measurement), 7th dimensional androgynous beings when the 7th dimension on the planet was the current vibrational frequency, it was a quite natural occurrence. They lived fully aware of their metaphysical connection to All and Gaia was rooted in their very nature.

THOTH

It was here where I would cross paths with and befriend the soul known as Thoth while in his initiate stages in Lemuria. He and I in those incarnations came up together as initiates of the Melchizedek priesthood. Our mentoring into that wisdom would be mirrored for our own overall Mastery but Thoth as you know followed an even Higher path when he was selected by The Dweller to continue his more advanced training to one day replace The Dweller as overseer of the planet. Thoth, myself and others would achieve the level of Melchizedek High Priest and I would serve as Priest / King in different places along the way. Thoth and I would remain close throughout our incarnations – dedicated to Earth and her ascension to Gaia. He was deemed the Protector of Gaia, and in his absence I would assume the responsibility until his return. I had always considered myself the best #2 on the planet throughout my life in different career roles ... and now I know why. My heart core mirrors Thoth's in that we are dedicated to the planet especially now while she is going through her final stages of evolution into the next dimension of higher frequencies. That's not to say that we don't have a heart for humanity – we love you, but our laser focused attention and resources are on the planetary ascension. I can guarantee every soul that – that measure of humanity who vibrate at the proper frequency (that which matches Earth's higher frequency) will indirectly benefit as a result. Your complete awareness of New Earth when the time comes will be sudden but you can be prepared. Only your vibratory level will matter.

When the Lemurians flourished they assumed responsibility over the grid work on the planet. Each one of the strategically placed 12 Crystal Temples connected by the 7th dimensional grid was assigned a Melchizedek High Priest King and High Priestess Queen (typically Twin Flames) to oversee the metaphysical advancement of their colonies. I was honored to be assigned to one of these Lemurian Temples by Thoth himself, but it wouldn't be my last outpost. This was prior to the development of the Atlantean faction you might say, who you could think of as a splinter group – originally Lemurian. They were interested in the more physical environment on earth – that is what they wanted to explore as opposed to the more spiritual nature of existence chosen by the Lemurian Melchizedek mindset. But they also were influenced by service-to-self beings who believed that lower forms should be brought under sway – where the Lemurians believed those Tribes should be supported as connected, but left to their own evolution as per the Law of One.

So here is where the Atlanteans began to migrate eastward from the area that was Mu-Lemuria, once land-massed quite differently in what we recognize as North, Central and South America today. In order to experience physical human form on the 5th dimensional plane a change in consciousness would need to be reached – so the Atlantean faction dropped to 5th dimensional awareness – one where physical form on the planet could be manifest and experienced. However, limitations on access to previous akashic records above the 5th dimension would be realized and the lessons of duality would commence.

I chose to stay on the Melchizedek path within Lemurian culture and keep a vigil on the cosmic progression of Light. I served in the final role Thoth had assigned me at one of the 12 Crystal Temples. This energetic crossing was on Lemurian territory which happened to be bordering immediately adjacent Atlantean territories until the final sinking of the major Atlantean colonies. Then I joined Thoth to the Land of Kem where we would take what we found there – primitives with remnants of Lyran / Pleaidian designed energy pyramids and fashion the next civilization to become Egypt. It would be administered over 16,000 years under Thoth's tutelage and wisdom sharing until it was to be handed over to humanity and the age of the human Pharoahs began. Thoth remains in the 8th dimension here as he is the Protector of Gaia, until sometime when he would return again as recorded in the Emerald Tablets.

SOLARIANS, CHARIOT OF THE SUN AND GOLDEN TAYA ALLOTMENTS

Toward the end of his physical presence on the planet Thoth began to organize the overseeing of its continued metaphysical advancement for Earth, by assembling the Merkabah group 'Chariot of the Sun' of which I honorably serve. The time would arrive when we would coordinate work with the Solarians during the upcoming LP-40 ascension process on preparing to activate Golden Taya territories.

[The Golden Taya Allotments are the areas of Earth's surface which will be ascending through the veil into the fifth dimension at the period of time referred to as Light Principle 40 (LP-40) by Tehuti/Thoth and his Merkabah group "Chariot of the Sun". According to Tehuti, the currently projected occurrence of LP-40 will fall somewhere between the years 2015 and 2025.

On February 17, 1995 we were experiencing some very powerful, yet strange dynamics. This prompted us to go to Tehuti and ask what was going on, as there seemed to be an unidentifiable component in the energy we were experiencing that day. Tehuti replied that this was the first day of the 'passing of the guard' of some of the Golden Taya areas from the control of the fallen lords (Nephilim) of light to the true Lords of Light (Solarians). He indicated this process would be occurring until approximately March 12, 1995 for the initial 20% of the Golden Taya Allotments.]

Upon his departure post- the Lemurian and Atlantean catastrophe periods, Thoth had left behind his Emerald Tablets – a resource recorded for those capable of interpreting its contents. It was meant for humans to understand for future purposes – basically embracing the existence of multidimensionality. Each of the twelve sections was given to one of the 12 High Priests to carry as signatures of Thoth's authority while they recolonized in 12 areas spread throughout the planet. It should be noted that each of the 12 Emerald Tablet sections were also embedded in Light codes and held within a corresponding Crystal Skull, this experience comes from my memories within my auric field. My Atlantean reawakening would be with the Mitchell-Hedges skull and my reconnection to Atlantis would be reactivated.

INNER EARTH (AGARTHA)
Some of these Taya territories would be on the surface especially for humanity's continued evolution but much would be located in Inner Earth locations, the entirety of which is referred to as Agartha. With over

120 different cities representing Lemurian and Atlantean cultures as well as other cultures we are not yet familiar with. They all await reconnecting with the surface in service according to the Law of One and holding that space to assist the lower density humans ascending through their own evolutions. You have heard many accounts of higher dimensional beings appearing and leaving behind higher technologies to assist those beings during that period of planetary recolonization.

I returned to this realm at this time, to watch over the Lemurian / Atlantean territory that I oversaw – it has an Inner Earth presence to this day beneath Lake Titicaca. This had been a unique place on the planet as both Lemurian and Atlantean influences and cultures had thrived here when both occupied this area together. It was a model of cooperation, unity, community and Light. It marked a time when all sentient life was truly connected as One. I know the energy from that sensation and I am eager to return to it. That is my purpose for this incarnation now – to do everything within my power and resources to ready returning humanity to the incoming higher frequencies of Light from the Melchizedek Law of One perspective of New Earth's elevated vibration.

We're almost there Lightworkers. ☐☐

So what are the signs of greater assistance from higher realms now and what evidence is there of the changes in earth's consciousness ...

It's important to start by knowing that during the Earth experiment in humanity – outside galactic influence was not permitted in order to allow humans to evolve on their own. Consequently, interactions with humans was forbidden. Clearly those cosmic orders were ignored by both beings on planet and off. Until the time of the harmonic convergence it seems to me energetically, the dark energies from off-planet had influenced and taken advantage of the human race for their own agendas. It was at this evolved stage of ascension that the frequencies with which those dark entities were allowed to experience Earth were no longer open to them.

'DISCLOSURE'
If you have done much research on the timing of the presence of the first so-called UFO sightings – you know this phenomenon largely began to be reported in the 1940's. There is good reason as to why ... as it was at that time period during WWII that we were developing nuclear weapons, testing them on US soil and consequently dropping them on an opposing country. Never mind the disregard of the Law of One with others that was being ignored ... humans demonstrated to higher realms what physical damage we could do to the planet, forgetful of the notion that the planet doesn't belong to us. Now that I have reminded you of the circumstances by which dark influences took down Lemuria and eventually Atlantis, you must see the parallels in lessons we didn't master.

What is different now, is that Earth as a planet, is at the final stages of evolving to a new higher vibrational plane where the 3D experience is no longer our reality. Where we are headed back to the Angelic Realm in the 4th dimensional version of Gaia while we skip on to 5D consciousness for all sentient life here.

That is the time higher dimensional beings started stepping in and making contact. If you are familiar with Dolores Cannon's work you already know about the three waves of volunteers who came to assist with Gaia's ascension beginning in the early 50's. I am one of the Blue Ray children who chose to incarnate at this time to assist with the imminent cosmic evolution of Earth and prepare humans for the transition.

The timeline of Earth's cosmic cycle in the 3rd density is closing, there is physical evidence galore of the catastrophic events taking place during this readjustment. Floods, wildly fluctuating temperatures, earthquakes, volcanic eruptions, solar flares, electrical disturbances, etc ... all triggered by elevated solar conditions in our system, emitted from a higher vibrational Photon energy belt of our Central Sun. Welcome to the actual Age of Aquarius and Golden Age. It's Earth's turn to evolve and you chose to be here to experience it.

During this time, many are coming into awareness of their Higher Aspects and seeing the world for what it is. They are also aware of benevolent higher dimensional beings here to help navigate these changes in cosmic energy. These guides have been around the planet, protecting it (and us), staying in their high vibration environments in Inner Earth as well as off-planet for this time. Communication like mine in real-time in Telos and other Inner Earth territories will be accelerating to prepare humanity with the location of vibrationally safe areas on the planet during the physical changes associated with rising vibration. Then the bridges nurtured by Earthly ambassadors with Beyond Earth Sentients over the past few years will become more widely acknowledged and accepted to pave the way for interaction.

3D SOUL CONTRACTS / LESSONS
Souls choose to evolve from within a 3rd dimensional plane to help Source understand more about itself in a setting of duality. The

soul will experience physicality in an environment of your choosing, learning both good and bad aspects in order to discern contrast. You will observe / record these instances into your personal Akash along your journey with your particular lessons. To rejoin with Spirit, share Akashic wisdom with the collective and choose to either ascend to the next level or agree to a new soul contact with new 3rd dimensional lessons to contribute through another incarnation.

New Earth has completed it cosmic schedule of 3rd dimensional lessons.
On we go to the next level where you're more likely to feel this density.

Namaste Starbuck

2023 Nov - Dimensional experience - visit energetic temple site in southern Telos territory, experienced Light beings on the property and went Lightbodied during a fire circle, Wisdom Spirit Ranch AZ

2023 Nov - Rion and I had a chance to exchange a bit one on one. He reminded me of my other roles when addressed me as Commander.

Made in the USA
Las Vegas, NV
08 November 2024

11308169R00216